THE MYSTERIES OF MODERN RELATION

THE MYSTERIES OF MODERN RELATION

Atul Kumar Pandey

KALPAZ

ISBN: 978-93-5128-092-7

Price: ₹ 120

First Published, 2015

Published by

Kalpaz Publications
C-30, Satyawati Nagar,
Delhi-110052
Ph. : 9212142040
E-mail: kalpaz@hotmail.com

Laser Typesetting : Quick Media, Delhi
Printed at : G. Print Process, Delhi

Cataloging in Publication Data—DK
Courtesy: D.K. Agencies (P) Ltd. <docinfo@dkagencies.com>

Pandey, Atul Kumar, author.
The mysteries of modern relation / Atul Kumar Pandey.
pages cm
Novel.
ISBN 9789351280927

1. Indic fiction (English). I. Title.

DDC 823.92 23

To my countery and
culture which call me for writing
about a truthfull story

The Mysteries of Modern Relation
Virginity is our
Dignity
A story about, Destroying Indian Relation,
Love for mint, money, prepare for
commission in the Armed forces, and blind love.

Preface

The mysteries of modern relation is a very unique master peace for Today's youngster's for their global modern relation, a relation between lovers and their beloved and husband's and wife brother and sister, uncle and their Niece and our friend every relation is very precious in Indian society. And further it is also it's master peace spreading a strong social massage against every corrupt relation of earth, against their culture custom tradition and relation.

How westerns culture spreading with full of motion in Indian society and it's polluted to unique Indian culture custom tradition and relation.

It's a story a about how a young man well educated in metro city of India's upcoming Army Officer's searches a well virgin life partner in remote village of India with a great expectation where who could got a unique well character virgin girl according to Indian culture custom and tradition that where before marriage loosed virginity chastity is against to Indian culture.

Now a day's metro city of India's fully adopted a western culture in the sense of enjoy.

They loosing their virginity chastity before the marriage, virginity is a precious important magnetic thing for Husband's and wife lover and their beloved.

The spoil of chastity and virginity becoming a main reason for breaking the relation in today society, be a loyal for your partner and be a happy for your life.

So young man searched a well character virgin beautiful and well educated girl in remote village of India how who was fell in the pure love with that girl she was poor but have star's like eye's her eye's was so killing and very beautiful structure.

How the young man awake many night in the pure love of beautiful girl, a young man loved her more but how gradually knows that beautiful girl was not well charactered have sexually relation with her real uncle, the young man loved her more than any other lover of earth and what happen when who knows that poison like realism.

What is going on Indian culture due to financial crisis a niece served her uncle as a prostitute.

Her uncle spend the money not for their blood relation, but for their sexually satisfaction.

Her mother and everyone in the family aware about their hated activities, but no one argue to old man why what is the value of money above than a dignity of Indian girl.

How much cheap cast the expense of our country girl.

One side's politician's full fill their bank and one side's a unique, beautiful, virgin, chasting girl loosed her shy, dignity, chastity, virginity only for money where is our social reformer and where is our law scholar.

And many incident read with carefully of this master peace.

Atul Kumar Pandey

Acknowledgement

I wish to thank, my mother, Smt. Sudami Devi, for my most unusual upbringing and for her constant message to me "you can do it". I am also supremely grateful to my father Late sub/Major Ramkripal Panday his sacrifices for nation was great, that always motivated to my carrier and for me his love for their three child—Asha, Reeta and Atul is unparalled. He is our backbone till the end of our life.

I am so also grateful to my two sisters Smt. Asha Tripathi and Reeta Tripathi for their love for me as a small baby and my three small nephews and Jijaji and my charm friend Chowdhary Baljeet Singh Beniwal he always are with me more than as a brother. I am also supremely grateful to my professor and as a elder brother Sir Umesh Chowbey.

—Author

About the Indian Culture

Today western culture, custom and tradition spreading with full of motion in Indian society and its pollutated Indian culture, custom, tradition and relation. Like what is the value of virginity. Virginity is a dignity of Indian culture, custom and tradition and relation is a main source of happiness in the Indian society. But its decreasing day by day. Today youngster loosing their virginity before the marriage its total against to Indian culture, custom and tradition. Youth should be utilise their energy in right path like education, sports, politics, entertainment it will be asset for the devolpment of their self and their country. They should be preserve their virginity till the marriage.

Because its a main expensive magnetic thing for husband and wife if they have earlier relationship with other. They have nothing new in each other and sex is the only thing they get as a new pure experience from each other. This must be pure and this must be **holly.** They should be preserve this expensive thing for their life partner because according to Indian culture sex is very secret thing. It should be share only with husband and wife. Its not a source of enjoy in Indian society. It is a trust of life partner every youth having a great expectation and hope to their life partner to preserve this expensive thing so do not deceive your life partner because only for enjoyment of some time do not make a question marks on your Indian culture. Because enjoy is temporary but pride is forever **Preserve Your Virginity and Preserve Your Culture.**

Story Beginning

My university, Punjab University Chandigarh, is a university of love and accumulate million stories every year, which is beginning in campus such as some turn into marriage and some made a memories for life time. I was misfortune regards love because I had no excess time for someone because I was student of B.Sc. medical science and cadet of N.C.C. but my mostly friend fell in love they were over in relation with some one. Many friend's latterly became a Army Officer, famous stars in bollywood and other migrated in abroad for further studies but after graduation my ambition was commissioned that's why India is the best option for me.

I was deserving cadet in second Chandigarh Battalion. I wanted to join Camp in O.T.A campus, it's a special camp. Their were many cadet applied for that but I was recommended for camp it's a 20 day's of camp which was held in Comptee Nagpur government offer me ticket of III A.C. of both side it's a special camp of personalities development and learned about officer's like Quality. I began my journey from Chandigarh to Nagpur. I arrived Nagpur in early morning it was my first experience of South Western India. That was the time of November but climate of Maharashtra was not cool it's a moderate type of climate. We stayed in barack (mean dulelling Royal Residence). It was nice experience each and every faculties is available here and we feel like as an officers we learned here good leadership quality and every compulsory partical which is need for combat officer. I was very great to achieve that great experience of my life. I was alonely represent Chandigarh Battalion. We were awaked in early morning 4 o'clock after fresh we were began our running of 5 km meter than came to the barack and did brush than take break fast after taking break fast we were take rest of 20 minutes after that started our training procedure full day. We were participated in group discussion weapon's training and group task obstacle when sun arise and sunset. We don't had time to think about that until we returned in barack at 6 O'clock in evening. that time we Feel like we came from a war became very tired I was single and don't have any girl friends. Once upon a time they offered to watch a adult movie that name was "An officer and gentleman" it was fully adult movie after watching movie our colonel bahuguna came in Auditorium and asked how much guys have their girl friend 70 per cent replied in favour of him but 30 per cent had no. I was also involve in them I lived a bachelor life.

He was trained as and ordered as make a girl friend go ahead infront of girl and purposed them if they will accept that's fine otherwise don't worry. After 20 days of training.

I came back to return in Chandigarh I secure twelfsth Secured 12 position in 98 cadet officer's were told me I am fit for Armed forces became glad. I arrived in Chandigarh November 2008 with commitment of make a girl friend.

I am a tourist by nature I like hill station and cool climate. I travelled in Shimla many times after training 12 February, 2009.

I was in Shimla. I sat in national coffee house Shimla at mall road, at my forward sit a fair a with curly hair passes smile she was quite and beautiful girl suddenly I was seen in her eyes. She also looked in my eyes.

I mispointed to my eyes but remembered that colonel was told me it's also a part of (officer's like quality). I was concentrate in her, eye and she don't mispointed to my eye so I also passed a smile and drooned in her eye. I feel she wanted to told me some thing I feel she accepted me her eye was told me she was very beautiful her lips are totally coral rosy red cheeck and good height thin waste (slim).

She looked in my eye and began to walk from coffee house she leave coffee house. I was also began walk behind her near about 200 metre I was followed her, she arrived at bus stand. I was also stand besides the bus stand. The bus was coming soon. I was asked her hello mam. She came back and asked me yes sir how I can help you and I feel you follow me from coffee house. I passed smile and replied that actually I am from chandigarh so I am an aware from Shimla and don't have any friend so if you don't mind can you guide me in here.

She replied evening is coming soon but don't worry I will help you for visiting many famous place she was offered me expensive 1½ hour's I visited whole mall road Lakkarh Bazar and other some where within 1½ hour, evening is turned into night.

I requested her for take dinner she was depressed but accept that we walked on road thousand of couple walk on road after seen them. I came near her name was Nicee Sharma she was from Shimla. (Sharma is Punjabi Brahaman)

I was very close with her she surprise I told her your company is comfortable for me please tomorrow once come and I will stay her with last seven days she was told me for come day after tomorrow the climate was very freezing night so I could not stopped and I was stucked her she awake and reply leave me every one is waiting for me at my home after dinner I proposed her regard's I fell in the love after 10 minutes of silence she accepted my proposal. I was asked her a kiss she sucked my lips and than she valediction to me after that I returned at my eazy guest house I was flying in the sky.

After 2 day's in Feb was my 21st birth day's that night was very pleasant night climate was very freezing after arrived in eazy Guest house I was sleep with very comfortable take wimpled veiled blanket at the above of my neek atmosphere of Shimla night was great. I had no any affection to niecee Sharma but as a young boy I had a sexual desire with her, but she was very beautiful that's why I do not wanted to leaset her belief on myself but that night I was drooned about her physical affection. But I never fell in love with her. She was offered me her contact number. I was talk to her near about 30 minute of became very warm that night but I have no another option for me that freezing night turn into very warm for me. I never did master bation so I drunk plenty of water and tryed to sleep after many difficulties. I was in sleep in early morning I was awaked in 9 O' clock in the morning an seen she were made 26 time call me. After fresh to myself and brush take bathed I was made a call for her she was very angry and told me for that idle. I was try to convince her she asked for came with me I was very nervous because I was virgin that time I had no any experience about the girl. I mad cawl name her that many friend came from Chandigarh regard celebrating my birth day I was told her for dinner party tomorrow.

That time a pure handsome vergin boy on the way of moulding in favour of a girl.

I was hanging in the compulsion of young age made many call to my charm friend like Chowdhary Suryadeep Singh Beniwal, Nawab Khan, Nitish Kumar Rai told that situation regard's my dignity virginity and exitance on the dispute they were suggest these all your thing have need destroy because it's a great time and great chance do not be to your self. Enjoy to tomorrow it's a special gift of your birthday which is offered by god. I cut the call and think many time about it's because. I was habitual of traditional and cultural life of Indian society and reverend the people of high moral that time I was learned by my family. So I was miss pointed sapana replaced niecee Sharma. But she was began to made me many call I could not received her call but due to impact of young age I was fail down to control my self and I think it's not her fault. I think every woman enters into one of the four elements to which her affinity is most and that time I was her super element how days was converted into evening in evening. I was leave eazy guest house and began to walk for evening climate was very cool so I was weared the woolen and tried to walk on hilly road atmosphere was great it's a influence of hundred of couple on the mall road and I stand beside infront the statue of Indira Gandhi. I alonely came the Shimla for visit and always I made single journey for hill station because in alonely journey. I was Liberate for visit and if we preferred in cluster so we could not admire according to our desire and in my case I am very tourist type of guys basically Natural vegation and cool climate is praise my heart and environment of hill station is a mingle of favorable for scholar and people who want to live some peaceful life to the Hot and rush climate of north and south plain it's totaly different experience to the crowdy plain. In hill station the people fully utilizing their time in favour of them and the capital of hilly state is more develop because Britishers prefered cool climate that's why they developed the capital of hilly state and according to my experience Shimla is more develop Than other north Indian hill station.

In the visiting of journey. I had visited the many Aristocratic people and family Which is a proud of emperor of hill station shimla. But do not anticipate the people under poverty line because their contribution and service for other upper and middle class is a unparalleled. I was socked at every morning whenever I watched that many people who came under poverty line do not made noise or wasted their time as a idle or made propoganda for their poverty line They lived Rustic life with smile. They did work hard with discipline you can not imagine that they tied gas cylinder over burden on their back side of body and run swiftly on side of body the pot hols and hilly road. At Shimla they provided cooking gas cylinder at every dwelling by him self it's their compulsion of poverty so I could not ignore it. It's a kind of white lead straightline, (part) represented gorgeous and behind lower part is ugly.

But the behave of locality is ring the bells and friendly. Whenever I travelled at hill station always I prefered visited in evening because in evening time modern hills station look like a paradise so in the Shimla that evening I standed at in front of the statue of Indira Gandhi that was very bonfiers (to enjoy in heart) I slowly began to walk on Mall Road, Mall was fully well decorated and I was became guidest lover's of my self so I was enternly very delighted and full that Mr. Atul Kumar Pandey is his chiefest height and my heart was enternal praise. Now the Mr. Atul Kumar Pandey turn to young boy's of the Shimla celebrated the boy in great joy with the first effection with Nicee Sharma in Shimla with her call and dream so day was turn into evening and in evening I was began the walk on rocky naturally beautiful road of Shimla that time my target was Mall Road visit and dinner, so I was slowly walking on Mall Road in front of church and statue and anima theatre.

I visited every decorated shop and restaurant and grooming over the expensive clothes but I had limited expanse the couplet is tighter but further it is also I am not addicted in fashionable vices or exhibition so it's a smooth and natural change that spended time our the expensive restoraunt because I able to effort for that and after the meeting with her the Shimla was more beautiful and I was in prison of a woman who are good but not cultured but soft and delicate by nature fully embrace with her beauty. She was totally opposite like a woman, who pretends to be more modest and moralist, than she really is I mean not she was flirts. But I am not sure about her chastity but acording to Indian culture custom and tradition and custom my wishes was about her chastity was compulsry I hope every Indian approved my decision about her chastity. It's a special gift of Indian society. I thought that how she could came very close with me in first meeting it's not our tradition but I convinced to my self about her chasting and convence to my self like she came because. I show by exciting manner's the hard-hearted ladies incline toward's the advances of men she thought that is their sense of honour which save the woman (from the advances of men) my empty mind think that rejected her artificial love. I feel that she could corrupt me. But my one mind increases offers of love I thought that in our ancient time chasting woman equipped with all the war arms against male and they improve his thought against woman. But I fell down to convence to my self and invokes to niece eyes after make up becomes all the more sparkling her eyes become as shining the lighting her terribly charming.

I was thought alonely at the mall road she was fashionable ladies she charms every looker-on my previous night and that night Atul Pandey laid on the alter of cupid made of twelve romance I was on the highest region of the sky because it's my first affection to any girl and I was dance excitedly at the thought of a fashionable youth that night every restaurant opened for entertainment by food and drink. But these all restaurant deceived by a lover Atul Pandey it was mist night very damp and chilly the mist was heavy but its a paradise for tourist and every tourist began to gathered on mall road because in light show shining as a moon shining in the million of star in sky. Heavy mist is an ornament of hilly capital shimla.

The tourist started to enteed in Aristocratic hotels and restaurant for enjoyed that paradise night and every rastaurant played extremely sweet, so sweet as to milt the heart captivating and soft sounds as they spread softly vanish along the surface of the great Himalayas mountain gentle west wind touches our chick and the colour of our chick turn into red snow which was very beneficial to the tilled field of apple in winter of Himanchal Pradesh. It's a great source of income of people of Himanchal Pradesh mostly economy depends upon the apple because its growing in the largest amount at the highest peack of Himanchal Pradesh and its to expensive than other fruit of Himanchal Pradesh. So every people was very praise. So night was shining mountain coverd with snow. I was in Indian cofee house with alonely so suddenly my cell was began to beeping. I was picked the call it was Nitish Kumar Rai did B.Tech from Chennai. Called me regard's wishes my birthdays. I was so glad Nitiesh Kumar Rai was my class mate in 12 and my good friend. He was from my districk we discused about our earlier day's in erlier time Nitish came from Chandigarh for take admission in B.Sc. (Honour's) in B.tech. for further studies we came from a rular area's that's why our Clothes was not similar than urban people we did not know's about many brand. Nitish came after my Admission he was stayed with me some time in hostel with illegaly but due to rumour of red of police we stayed in a lodge. But many people made a vulgar joke about his clothes and a simple sate mobile in campus he was always hurted by students my room mat Vishnu Chandra made a vulgar comment but Nitish could not control to himself and Cwerell with him and I was tried to control their cwerell. I was convince them and laterly they accepted their mischeif behave against Nitish. I was very aggresive against my room mate Vishnu so I made a called my class mate and good friends Dhananjay Atary, Dr. Vimal Bamal and Ganga boora these all are came in my favour ready for fight with my classmate and their some friend's so in evening we all of one gatherd on infront of sourya bhawan, sourya bhawan is very holly palace because my college build a statue every defence officer who was martyr in action as well as in peace, their statue spread the full of energy and proud for its every student, these all officers pass out from my college.

Captain Vikram Batra is also pass out from my college who was hero and martyrs of kargil war in 1999. and a winner of highest gallentry award P.V.C offerd by government of india highest galentry award Paramveer Chakra, Major Sandeep Sagar and many.

The ownar of Sahara Subrat Rai and Ex-Captain of Indian cricket team Mr. Kapil Dev, Golfar, Jeev Milkha Singh S/o. star Atheletes Milkha Singh, youngstar cricketar Yuvraj singh and bollywood star Ayushman Khurana these all are great presonalities in their different field but one thing is comman in these. These all are alumunus of D.A.V. College Chandigarh where I was studies sector 10D its a heart of Chandigarh and whole North India.

Their are great environment for every student for their different field like N.C.C. for those who want to be a I.P.S. or Army officer Agaz for those who want to represent the bollywood as a film star. Great cricket ground with excellent coach. Cricketar of Indian cricket team like Yograj Singh or Dinesh Mongia and decorated South Indian Coffee House in our compus the shop of fruit and fruit juice its makes to their student to more energetic hostel provided good quality of meal. Which is very healthy for its student health you can say hygine food provided for its student so their are fcr four hostel for it's student New hostel, Himanchal. I hostel and Himanchal II and B.T.C. hostel means Bakshi Tek Chand hostel good and knowledge full library where every types cf book available large number of amount of books where every ambitious student take time for their future war generally the behave of people of North India is freindly and brotherhood they are very helpfull for their surrounding people and very supporter they are not practical they live very comfortably and peacefully life. They are pure Aryan's because they look like western Asias and south european people I am so also a part of them our looking is same but they are more fair and good hight as well as the people of eastern north Indian U.P., Bihar but further it is also easily and I use could acclimatriee to myself in that environment the climate of Chandigarh is very extremely pleasant not to hot and not to freezing. Its a moderate types of climate but winter is much cool than other south or middle part of India but one thing is beneficial for this region that is no one die by weather calimaties, because it like it's basic apply in my native place like north east U.P. and Bihar many people would be die because due to the poor infrastructure and due to poverty problem they are enable to maintain their clothes in winter that is why the people spoil their life but Chandigarh having every people who could effort for basic fundamental requirement the like they easily can change their clothes, Acording to climate they are rich and hard worker they knows their value.

Our college canteen is also a place of noon meeting blunder situation happend or some thing special meeting need for the stdudent that time cofee house was best place. For thought ful student they were discuss about every serious are current matter in the cofee house coffee house was situated in enternal campus of our college bat but canteen was situated in external part of our college. The hostal was a dwelling of every outsider student my hostal represented. The whole india, its a influence of every student of different state Kashmir to Kanya Kumari (Tamilnadu), Mizoram to Guzarat every state minimum contribute to one student for the hostel West Bengal to Kerela, and Maharashtra surrounding of college is very pure nature is to close to my college and every student who study in D.A.V Sector 10 D.

Actually that night happened what about Nitish and my Room mate Vishnu due to rumour of the raid of police. I stayed Nitish with in lodge. It was a time of night but we were not sleep. Nitish was seat and my head was on his lap of Nitish. We were talk to each other about our future. He wanted to became a rich person and I was ambitious for commisson in the Armed forces suddenly my cell phone was beeped. Nitish was picked it was a SMS by unknown number SMS in comes the word. Mr. Atul Kumar Pandey you are so hot I want to spend one night with together. I was shocked. He was admire and asked me regards it I was replayed that. I do not knows any girl who could this type of SMS me. So he was replayed that sure I would also like and I do not know really what he was replied her but I was advised him for do not make any mistake by your self and I was sleep and he late night chated with her next days we moved in hostel because our luggage was keep in hostel. So when we enterd in my room No. 56 my room mate Vishnu Chandra, asked me Pandey why you sms to my girl friend I was replayed that I do not knows the mobile no. of your girl friend so how it may be possible. So I understand about previous night SMS but it was a fault of his girl friend. She was sms me and told him for that I was made her a call for talk to her so Nitish was replayed that its a mistake of your. I was tryed to covence them and I was told him that its a fault of your girl friend because I have no cont. n. of her how it may be possible regards talk to her but he all ready. Aggressive collected the some friends in favour of him like Yusuf and one or two more they were told me that, Pandey ji its your fault suddenly Nitish and my room mate cwerell with each other and both tried beat each other and I tryed to stop them they abused to each other laterly I convince them and I tried to convence that they are in majority laterly Nitish was not approved my decision he made the argument to me that we should be coordinate with them finally I succeed in advised him he was approved my decision so three days we stayed in lodge and I was bunk the classes but the my many class mate made me call regard's bunk the classes but I ignore them but Dhananjay Atary and Vimal Bamal is my good friend so I was told the situation of Vishnu Chandra and his blame. I was fearless but due to Nitish admission I could not take time, they were told that report of the Sourya Bhawan.

We reported at Shourya Bhawan. I was convince the dhananjay, for call the Vishnu for Shourya Bhawan and I was very aggressive that evening.

They came with a clustar of Punjabi boy's suddenly Dhananjay call to Haryanwi so, large number of Haryanwi came in favour of us as. But we try to keep the situation with in both gang, because many panjabi was our friends so laterly they abused to my room mate both gang abused them and their mischief against as laterly I stand to beat the Yusuf Nawaz. He was accepted his fault and touches my feet, told that Pandey ji It's my blunder mistake. But really I do not know what is going to realy happened. I abused to every one who made me for call his blame girl friends laterly Vishnu understood the realy situation that it's a fault of his girl friends and he was appologised for that we compromise that and laterly we become a good friend. My room mate was became very caring for me after that incident. I thought about his girl friend character to how she could SMS me this type what is her custom. I was advised his girl friend if she do not improve about her mischeif character some thing would happen to very dangerous with her not by any people by nature because its not our tradition, Only not in three year in Chandigarh. It was an incident of I year, but till the final exam of Vishnu of III year, his girl friend father made sucide and sarrow of a husband death her mother could not suffer and laterly she made a another sucide to her self. Its a very dangerous, incident which was happend, only with in few year, but who was responsible for her father or her mother or she is her self is fully responsible for that a girl who is in pure love with some one fully embraced with some one and other hand she made a vulgar SMS to another boy's Mr. Pandey you are so hot and I want to spend one night with together what is this.

I was in very young age came from rular India but basically from upper middle class rich Brahaman family. I was learn calture in family I was civilized. My room mate spended more money for her presonal requirement he was in love with her but she made vulgar mischief so you all of you a better judge than me who is fully responsible for her parents death.

It's a Indian society. I think do not be a extremely practical for relation. Why you all of you becoming a follower of western society where is your custom and culture laterly Vishnu break up with her it was a long relation. how she could release to her self. What is she gain in relation. Nothing only losses, her father, her mother, her chistity (virginity) and main thing is that her honour dignity she made a hundred call to Vishnu but laterly she understood about her fault he was good manner boy released by her and laterly joined B.H.U for his further studies, but she had only tear, guilty and unknown question to herself for life time, no one is stand for convence her because she all ready loose to her real family if she firstly understood if, moral value of her honour chastity it may be she could saved her parents life and her virginity.

So Nitish spended more than two months with me but he came late so the seat of honour's in any subject streams was full that and he wanted to take admission in B.Sc. (biotech) it was earlier full down. I was convince him try for upcoming in next year Admission in B.Tech he was commited for work hard because he was very hurted by that incident and his dressing sence, so laterly he moved for Lucknow prepare for I.I.T. entrance exam, he did work hard and fully embraced sacrifice, with hard determined to his study, and laterly he became success, he could not qualified I.I.T. exam, but cleared

N.I.T. examination for B.tech courses he was joined Anna University in Chennai.

Became very serious for his studies well performs in his stream he choosed computer science, as a B.tech. try to work hard in their software studies even he was from a middle class family so he began to work as a counsellor and made 25 lakh rupees with in three years he purchase every expansive daily uses materilist thing because he all ready remembered the Chandigarh situation, he full fill his personal desire expansive mobile, expansive motercycle, expansive branded Laptop expensive branded cloths so what was happen with him every thing he was learn by society like student made vulgar joke against him. In Chandigarh for what, because he was came from, a rural area his cloths was not branded or superior as well as, a middle class or upper middle class of urban student, so society teaches him everything laterly he was became a integral part of our urban society.

Nitish moved Chennai for B.tech. engineering. I worked hard in b.sc. and specialy in NCC camp first. I joined A.t.c (Annual training camp) in 26 sector Chandigarh. I was represented my college as a Athelets I was good runner, and spended more time in physically exercise. It was a fourteen day's of camp and influence of every compulsory training for a combat officer we were follow that's all waked up in morning and began to a Journey of a day with five kilometer of running. than we take time for break fast only for twenty minute's than we concentrate on drill practise, drill is most important for a combat officer it's a symbol of discipline. Daily we spended more than two hours in a drill Practice, I was not good in drill but I was good runner, good shooter. Always I was represented my college in both field Athelets and shooting my every friend was very charming, like Chowdhary, Suryadeep Singh Beniwal, he was my class mate and NCC course mate, and Yatin Saroha, Chayan Chahal Saroha and Chayan was not my class mate but my course mate in NCC both guys are super laughter. Whenever we had empty time they made jokes on each and a other friend. Nawab Khan, Jagdev Yadav we were full enjoyed in the camp with tough exercise, but jokes and argument made it so easy. Once upon a time in a A.T.C. camp. I was good in my company so everyone has full reverenced for me at a time we practised about a dreal, we were learned thing particular, which is helpful for dreal that time our senior under officer, Paramdeep Singh Sahur laterly he was became officer by I.M.A. So that time he was our senior, and student of my college in B.A. III or M.A. I, and we were in graduation first year student he was, lead as.

Suddenly one hawaldar came and ask him how much you having good student, send them for office work, it's order of colonel sir, so he was orderd five student for maintain the some files, in five of them include me, we moved for office but subedar major sir stoped as in mid way and told that our duty was as a saffer mean they wanted cleaned the D.T.H. (D.T.H mean, A (bus) which having a large number of lating sheet, it's a good for environment and hygined so our duty was that clean the lating I was shocked because I never clean the dung fossil or lating of another person. I was cleaned the my laiting. It was sufficient for me, but S.M. Shab orderd as for clean the lating they were tried stand against the military rule but S.M. Sahab was told that Duty is duty, and you all of you want to be a officer so you have need aware about your surrounding dirt and dust and it's a dust of your friend so, it's your responsibility for cleaned it. I was told him that we want be a officer, not a saffer we spended money time learning hard for what clean the vichle toilet but he was told as a suppose that we hanged in a problem in a forest and surrounded by enemy and their are limited place and you all of you, having a majority of a officer so who would be clean your dirt, it's a stair of a combat officer training gentleman, becoming a officer is not so easy, so every four friend and S.M. Sir also involve in the clean of lating it's a first time for me but his order was reality laterly he was asked me about my cast when and he knows he was prevented me but tried to teach that it's our duty and every gentlemen cadet of I.M.A. and O.T.A. follow these instruction. I was silence in evening we return for our barrack where my every friend gathered whenever I arrived at barack Suryadeep asked me where you all of you maintain the file I was honestly told that every situation after receiving this message, my every friend became very aggresive against Paramdeep Singh, they were asked the question, why he involve me, in toilet cleaner he replied that he did not know about the realy what was commond he was knows only that they engaged as for maintain the register but I was also silence about it but my friend thought that Paramdeep Sir is a responsible for that suddenly the drop's of tear's came from his eye's and feel really apologize for that but no one in favour of him another days was a final competition of drill running and shooting. But best cadet was my good friend whose could made good performance against every college and Punjab university but they were not participated for that competetion. I was runed that days and secure good markes. I secured 8 position out of 88 cadet. D.A.V. 10 was well performance in athletes but defeated in drill after over the camp every one feel that fault. Mostly Paramdeep sir, no milldy away we came in college feel like young. G.C. It was, my first camp II camp was Army attachment camp which was held on western head command Chandimander, Chandigarh (U.T).

After first camp of A.T.C. every cadet became more discipline nawab was very colourful type of men who made many girl friend I always, advise him that, do not play to any one of life because it's no doult if you think you are more, wise so it's your fault because, main player, is a nature wherenever you think I am very clever and you would cheat the person, who realy trust on your self it's my prersonal experience that you would be hang in the problem of cheating by another you would be cheated by another person.

He enjoyed to his life but laterly he dispointed to his way he wanted became a Amry officer but addiction of his habit prevented him as a officer in Army so upcoming camp was Army attachment camp with 1/4 Gorkha rifles was very important camp for every because Gorkha rifles having a great history in Indian Army they are very dedicated, loyal honest and warrior they win many galentry award in action as well as in peace. In every war of Indian Army their contribution is unparallel they knowing for their knight type of attitude so the camp with gorkha rifles was very important that's why everyone cadet one wanted to join that camp. My senior all ready had earlier experience with Maharashtra infantry attachment camp in previous year.

But further it is also they wanted to joined that camp but seat was very limited their are only 18 seat offered by Army the number of my senior was fifteen but only eight on active for joined that one so they cancell the many name which one came from my batch because we were go junior of them they selected only handfull cadet which all was not superior but these all are in the favour of my senior they always stand for my senior, but that all are not good in running shooting dreal, and group discussion in these all thing, which is most important for a Active NCC cadet they are not well for that they were cancelled my name from main list in a one evening time. My senior under officer, Mayank Badotra cancelled the my nomination from main list and when. I was asked him for reason, he was told me that I am B.Sc. student and do not attend daily dreal. I told him that its a Army attachment camp their are every activities is most important for a cadet because suppose any soldier officer good in dreal and bad in atheletics and shooting so how they can win the war and it's a Army attachement camp and I think that I am good for that camp he was told me that it's a very tough camp and should be more deserve. I was replayed that every day's I completed twenty kilometre of running tough exercise and in Army attachment camp they should be only five kilometre of running so how, it may be possible that I can not deserve for that in the way accepted that I am not good in dreal but I am a brand in the world of Athlets for my college and always I represented the college and secured the good position the father of Mayank sir was (colonel) in J&K light infantry laterly Mayank sir, recomanded for. O.T.A. Chennai, and and got sword of honour, awarded by president of India, it's very laterly.

It was evening time of 8 Octobar 2008 every cadet gathered on infront of Shourya Bhawan my junior was practised for dreal and Mayank Badotra, sir was commanded them because he was our super senior and as a rank acording to NCC Rule he was our senior under officer that time my every coursemate of NCC who was realy my batchment and my other senior and Junior every one.

Attained because after four days the camp was coming soon which was held in western head command chandimandir Chandigarh laterly Vijendar Singh Gill sir came with a list which was nominated the some handfull cadet everyone was very ambitious for their name for that great camp. I was also but they cancelled the my namenation that day's was very hot for Mayank sir, because after declared the final list my every senior my course mate and my junior became literaly anger against my senior Sivendar Pandey Sir, laterly he recommended in O.T.A and became a Army officer argue with Mayank sir that with Atul is a deserving cadet so how you cancelled his nomination your list is totally fake you all ignore the deserving cadet. You should be prefer him he was replayed that he is deserving but not attended the daily drill and that list is totally depend on daily attendence not like other suddenly my every course mate withdraw their nomination against the mayank Sir list, I was asked Question to mayank Sir, that who is good runner he was told that Atul Pandey. I was told him infront of all my senior junior and my coursemate that sir, if you are good in dreal. I am good athelets they are two different activities but both having their different importance so. If you are ignore it so please come in ground and run with me and its my challange that if any your course mate my senior defeat me in running surely I would never join the camp it's very inferior word for mayank Sir, he fell, lost his dignity at in presence the all of them. He was unabale to says any word. I was told him that you are a B.Sc. student I am so also, he was told me that I am a S.U.O. of your, and I will see it. I warn them you all of you my senior. Mr. Atul Kumar Pandey and his good course mate would be join this camp and your list is fake list I would maintain the another list and you all of you never join this camp it's my commitment to all of you.

Next day's I was reported at II NCC Battalion Chandigarh that time my colonel was Nagar Dutta. I was told that every situation what was happened with the fake list that time our. Lieutiont colonel Bahtiya sir was very appreciate about my personalities and coloml Nagar Dutta sir, was also they were replayed that you are only fit for this camp you have a magnetic presonalities like a Army officer they were cancelled the fake list which was maintained by Mayank, sir, and parmoted me as a senior, under officer for this cam provide me commission me for this camp.

And offered forty new application form and that time I was beame a all in all virtual of NCC in my college. My every senior, defeated by my self.

Vijendar Sing Gill was told that we will see the performance of D.A.V. college commanding under new senior under officer, Atul Kumar Pandey.

He was announced that in previous camp D.A.V. could not win any medal and that camp represent by as. We would see Mr. Atul Kumar Pandey and their team.

My every friend was very charm and appreciate about our achievement against our senior.

Vijendar Gill sir was announced that our achievement would be nothing he twice remind the every cadet that our performance will be menial. But I was became a senior under officer of my company so I was provokes to every cadet regard's camp began un-tring hard work with all of them with jesting my every comreds began hard exercise. Running with zealously fully they wanted to well performance in upcoming comp because. My every senior protested to over involvement in this important camp lieutenant colonel Bhatiya sir, was announced that the limit of seat was laterly increases so it was a another overburden for recruit the more cadet limit of seat was increase fifteen to twenty five that time my many friend wanted to join the camp but they were sluggiss and anable to particpate in hard physicaly exercise and I had a overburden that, time I was the camp first time leaded so I was orderd them for began the hard exercise they were follow my command. My mentaility was select recruit that every cadet who are ambitious because ambition made untiring hard work. My every Comreds was very diligence but every one knows them as a sluggis. I was made a speech to infront all of them that. I leaded a company of my course mate comred's who having same experience as well as myself and a very handfull intelectual junior and two most senior so you all of you a S.U.O. and it's your responsibility for well consequence every one was in my convicing. I was mad a committment for welldone performance in upcoming camp my every comred's are very zealously for be a part of this camp. I made a very perspectivety word's for super consequence. Every cadet defended my speech and made a chivalry commitment for welldon performance they were determined. I recruited my coursemate Nawab Khan who was my good friend but sluggiss and romantic earlier my best friend Choudhary Suryadeep Singh Beniwal and Yatin Saroha did not wanted to recruit him but laterly they were defended my decision and Nawab was recruited as a cadet Nawab was also very determined for this camp he did not wanted to pluck this camp every one knowing that is Diamond opportunity of their life because the attachement of with Gorkha is very glory and opportunity of great fate. Indian Army is a Union of warrior and Knight. Every regiment having their great value they knowing about their great history. Every Infantry batalion participated in externally and internally defence, in war and as well as in peace they heaving their same value no doult these all are a indication of gallant. But Gorkha is specially warrior in Khukuree attack. They finished many enemy with their Khukuree without gun so they are specialist in Khukuree war and honesty and loyalty.

I had many close friends and in all of them Chowdhary Suryadeep Singh beniwal was special because he was my class mate and in NCC as well as course mate we had good understanding he was science student and well participated in sport's so I think it's happended in very rare cases that science student partcipated in fully sports because they do not have sufficient time for sports but I was also very interested in sport's always I was participated in athelets and secured good rank in my college because basically I was from rural areas. So habitual of sports I have sufficient time for sports at my dwelling that's a reson for good coordination between me and Suryadeep Yatin Saroha was also my good friend he was not my classmate but my coursemate in NCC and my good friend. We had also good coordination, easily could understood each one. Yatin was also ambitious for camp, that time I was single and also Suryadeep but Yatin was in love with Armani. She was from Dehradun. Yatin was in love, he was fell down with Armani in love. Yatin spiritually loved with Armani but Armani cheated him because she had a another boy friend she made him always fool, she was average not very beautiful many time friend advised him for leave her but Yatin was in spiritual love he made ten time of journey for Dehradun he always meet with her and tried to convince her for her loyalty with him she always commited with him for her loyalty but always through the masque of Indian girl. Who are specialy knows for their chasting and virginity, she lost her virginity with her previous boy friend in ninth class she was told to Amit. I was shock, Yatin was in the complusion of blind love he wanted marry with her.

She was only passed the time with Yatin was aware to her

every conspiracy but he did not wanted to abduction with her. Whenever he was perturbed talk with one about solution. I know she was not well for marriage by any angle when I watched the glowming face of Yatin. I was only twice the world that who could not care about her chasting, about her self so how she can care your self but further it is also if you want you can stay with her but as a good friend but not as husband or boy friend so he was continued with her with a hope of true love. I was advised Yatin that if any girl fell down in love and created a physically relation to any one before marriage so she will fill down always after the marriage in that case if her life partner suffering to any physicaly internally problem but if any preserve their virginity till the end of marriage I am hundred percent sure.

She will be wait her life partner till the cure treatment of her life partner so I was advised him for break the relation with Armani because Yatin's father was Sub-Inspector in Indian Tibetion boarder police force. Yatin was elder's in boys so he have a responsibility of his family and he was drawned in blind love with Armani that's why he would not well performance in every where laterly their relation came was on road of life they live happy with each other they mentain good coordination so Yatin was mentally prepared for up-coming camp that's which was held in Western Head Command Chandimandir, Chandigarh. Every one was free to the responsibility of life we are very chearfull and glad friend of the worlds that was a good performance in up coming camp my every comred's fully defended me and allivated my moral.

I was became very responsible person that time a praise came from my internal soul because I was busy for hard exercise. We had only one target and studies that tommorow build a combat officer. It was nice time of my life the previous love of my friend who had a great expectation to their self and more my self that we will success in our goal every one gathered for success in not only in upcoming camp but in also in their life. It was commitment of DAV. Ven student we had a great expectation to our self because, DAV. had a great history. So we remembered that about our senior and repoteation because that time the command of DAV. in our hand because we was feature of tomorrow of DAV. it's totally depend on our soldier's the dignity honour and a habit of win. Which is name of our college. Our college build the feature of tomorrow India so we had overburden and inspiration to our senior.

We prepared for camp dry cleaned our combat uniform and collect the our name plate it was specially made the our name plate if was specially made by 17 sector Chandigarh and collected woolen clothes because the camp started to the 18th october polished the shoes every one will knows about no any excuse possible in the up coming camp because we are mature graduate student of top institution of India.

They had great expectation to our majority. Every one fully engaged in preparation. Because they estimated that its a great opportunity of their life. They tried to speak fluently in english prepared for general knowledge and participated in group discussion tried to involve in hard physically exercise they fully disciplined did responsible their responsiblity shining on every one's face reverenced (respect) them because they choosed their tough life on the basis of their own decision they prepared for serve their own mother land they became fully patriotic. They wanted to became strong combat Army officer, Many cadet was weak by body they specially practise for their physically exercise and every one wake up in early morning because they fully concentrate on their personal performance it must for every one.

Every one knowning the value about their personal performance. Everyone having their own value it may be not possible that all one great in every activities but rare person was in all in one, like Chowdhary Suryadeep Singh Bewiwal basically me. Mr. Atul Kumar Pandey. Yatin Saroha. Every tryed to sacrifice and wanted made an impact in different activities. Like in some one practise for rope game. I was practiseing for running and shooting and Yashpal Punchel was specially practise for their drill (Laterly moved Canada for L.L.M.).

I was also good in studeies as well as in sports so I was practise for all round performance. So before camp I was inform to everyone that report at infront of shoury Bhawan every one gathered at 16th October. I wanted to share a great decision, that I was announce that I do not wanted to became a senior under officer because two other more senior is also attend there camp and they are very close to retirement from NCC I was convince to infront of every one that it I became senior under officer, so it may be possible that my individual performance may be effected by our overburden the responsibility of every cadet but my senior is all ready well perform in previous camp and they only wanted to join for their certificate but they are not very ambitious, so its our responsibility that offer him a chance of command and we should take a chance of command and we should be fully work in under their command what is their own decision and lastly.

I was told that a word I want to only 100% of performance to your self. So without any overburden do the hardwork. Every one silently listen and approved my decision, they became very appriciate about my decision.

I told them that it's our first Army attachment camp a first stair to proof your self. So do not take any overburden for tomorrow exercise. Give fully scrifice for it's every one was fully aggry to my decision. I made a call to Sivendar Pnadey sir. I was offer him a post of senior under officer he was told me that Atul you are all ready choosed for S.U.O. I was convence him that sir. (want to fully drooned in the performance, I did not wanted made any excuse, but if I became a senior under officer so it may be possible that if I could not well perform in the camp so it may be possible that I will be made a excuse of S.U.O. so I want to give fully perform in the camp without any excuse. Sivendar Pnadey sir was carefully listen about my decision and he was aggreed on my decision he was ready for responsibility of S.U.O. he was very appreciate about my decision and sacrifice for my upcoming camp. I was remind to every one that our senior wanted to see as a loosar. But I want to win in any condition. My every course mate, and junior became very serious about the camp they only listen by myself that I want to win and welldone perform in the camp in every or any condition. My senior was very crazy about our performance they wanted to judge our leadership in upcoming camp Actualy the invironment of DAV college in about NCC Cadet is not equal than other university or college. D.A.V college created a atmosphere of combat leader every cadet behave to their self as an officer not like NCC about because their target for tommorrow feuture so in 78 only recruited 25 cadet for Army attachment camp and it's a fortunately my two senior Sivendar Pnadey Sir and Komal Singh Sir was also a part of that camp laterly both became a Army officer, they journey of camp was began to 19 octobar 2008. Every Cadet cut their hair style as a Army Officer they cleaned save and every important luggage they collected for the camp. Nawab was breack relation to every girl for this important camp.

His confidence was shining on his face Daljeet Sing Dahiya and Brijesh Dhingra both are over haffty cadet but both are trying to reduce their weight they have over weight but thier confidence and moral was so high than a physical fitness their fatty body fully ready for tough to tough exercise they wanted to more better performance than a slim cadet their tendency was that fully scrifice and achieve the target. Every one had a aim for win. They do not wanted to loose their a single point for this camp Every one fell like a well responsible person of the Team. Daljeet Singh Dahiya and Brijesh Dhingra was not ready to accept their heavy body. Their confidence defeated their overburden body finally Sivendar Pnadey Sir. Became our Senior under officer. Actualy he was supported as in front of Mayank Sir. and other every senior, he was in the favour of his junior. He wanted to offer the opportunity for young cadet that's why we were decided to offer him a responsibility of S.U.O my one other senior was Komal, he was not interfere in previous junior selection. That's why my every course mate and my junior in the favour of both recomandation. Because Komal Sir was not joined previous camp which was held with maratha light infantry he was not participated in the junior selection he was in the favour of performance those who could they should be provide the opporunity. Komal sir and Vipul Pandey Sir was good mate. There were not classmate. But they were coursemate in the NCC and they had good coordination between each other. So their company was very experienced for as so we were happy.

Sivendar Pandey Sir was in B.Sc. III in Bio informatics. Bio- informatics is the branch of science that deals with study of information related Biology so he was prepared for C.D.S entrance exam. But he had N.C.C. and in upcoming year he would be got C certificate in NCC so he does not need to take the written exam he will getting for direct SSB. Komal Sir was also B.Sc. III student but he had a compartment in physics. So who have have a overburden of his studies one sides is N.CC camp and anotherside preparing for physics compartment exam so he had a some critical problem but laterly he passed in physics and recomanded in O.T.A. laterly became an Army officer both guy's we were happy because we all course mate a feat away from the reason of feature because we were junior of them and both our senior treated as brotherhood.

The camp was began to 19 October 2008 firstly an Army bus came in our college. Every cadet was in NCC uniform stand with their luggage besides the Sourya Bhawan we were waited for bus when bus was came in the college. Every one became glad bus was in fully military green colour with strong symbol of Indian Army and Khukuri cross it was a early morning time so every one was take the bananas and seap the fruit juice because it's not a break fast time near about 7 a.m. The bus came with a driver and two strong Army Jawan.

Suddenly they down from the bus and smartly they ordered us for take the seat every cadet was shake off to fear of the camp because they did hard exercise we seat in the bus with proudly that yes. Our destination is no long and began talk to each other when bus was started our S.U.O. Sivendar Pandey Sir stand at infront to us and cryed a patriotic slogan. Indian mother land we cryed that we salluted. The bus was running inslow speed he continued with the slogan, of Indian mother land we cryed that we salluted with seriously because we feel that we are real defender of our mother land. The bus running outside of our college gate. Our slogan was very soundly every one of our college student and member litsten our soundly patriotic slogan for our mother land. The bus was running from outside of the college gate.

The greenry and pleasent climate surrounded by the beautiful city which was situated in foothills of Himalyas. The bus was on the road every cadet made eye glance at outside of the window atmoshphere was so moderate. With in normal speed bus arrived at Matka Chowk. Matka Chowk is well decorated chowk. A chowk where four length divided. The Matka Chowk is a specially decorated by foreigner different varieties of flower's.

This type of the decorated chowk only designed in Chandigarh in whole. The atmosphere of Chandigarh is so unique and it's direct effected to human being's due to the impact of unique climate. Its locality is so healthy, smart, fearless and charming.

The climate of Chandigarh is favourable to do the hard work. So we crossed Matka Chowk and slowly – slowly our driver tried to elope with a jouney of future combat officer every one made eye glance at outside of the window. They are every appreciate about their decision because on the road. In royal city of India is Chandigarh our bus was running in many expensive car. Our bus was running on the road with normal speed but the bus was so different than other expensive car.

Our bus was not more expensive than foreigner car, but it

had it's different proud reverence and mose value and dignity. Many expensive car anabule to raee us.

Our bus not because their capsity was not so high or sealed their engine for race because their driver aware that it's a bus of our national defender. We were made eye glance at outside of window and read the face of people. They made us more eye glance than us because we were totally different and every civilian watches us with proudly a confidence and with true trust that in every critical time of the country they would ready for the safety, honour's and welfare of Indian motherland that's why every expensive car and vehicle did not had a guts for passed our bus because they understood that it's a very younger youth but they choosed a way and life of very rough and tough in the favour of Indian mother land. They would be save the nation so their respect is our first responsibility. Every one seat with proudly with a strong ambition of upcoming camp every cadet was very appreciate that after lot's of critical problem we are very close to our distination. The bus was in normal speed. We enjoyed with conversation to each other. The path was very comfortable. We crosing Chandigarh and enjoyed and made by glance at the out side of the window. The atmoshpere was incredible and read the life style of the people.

They fully adopt a western culture the city decorated with many park Garden and lake Rose Garden, it's very famous in world wide Rose garden is a secured first position in the Asia. The total garden decorated by foregheinar flowers the visitor coming from across the world wide. The garden is decorated by artificial rainbow and lake.

Sukhana lake is also famous in world wide This lake is totally paradise of the world and a great symbol of Architecture.

Sukhna lake is a artificial lake which is situated in foot-hills of Himalaya's it's a very peacefull place and influence of pure and unique air. the picture of Sukhna lake is auesome and it's a place where easily we can watches the real picture of middle Himalaya's.

Rock garden is also very decorated Artificial garden which was build by Bakshee Tek Chand. The every useless material of the city Bakshee Tek Chand was utilise in the rock garden and the whole garden is decorated by useless material of the city but easily no any could judge. So it's a main hot spot of Chandigarh. Sukhna lake and rose garden is very famous for young couple if some one in any problem but after preseve of Sukhna lake or rose garden the will be release their problem from and further it is also that the city decorated with many shoaping complex many branded clothes shop and shoping mall.

The people of Chandigarh lived in present they enjoyed every moment of their life. But one thing is demerit of their that they fully adopt a life of western culture it happening because it's a group of major people staying in western country so. Infavour of result they are adopting the tradition of western people and country. They resleasing the custom tradition and culture of Indian mother land. Slowly slowly our militry green colour bus shining on the road.

In Royal city of India in Chandigarh. It shining between many expansive car as well as moon shining in the sky between million of star's.

Slowly-Slowly we were reaching close to our target finally we were very close to the gate of western Army head command gate Chandigarh.

We were five hundred metres away from the western head command gate. Chandigarh every cadet made eye glance at the out side of window.

The gate was decorate by a strong symbol of great warrior's two Khukhri Cross and a strong symbol. Indian Army the picture of western head. Command gate was Avasome Incredibule we feel that. It's a Royal empire.

The gate was fully decorated in influence of knight warrior's scholar and wisdom.

The bus was a very close to the main gate easily we could watches the real picture of western head command. It was more delighted to our heart than imaginery picture.

The gate was a great symbol of a dwelling where dwelve our real national defender.

I seat in bus with Jagdev Yadav he was basically from Allahabad. But dwelling in Chandigarh. His father was clerk in our college he was charming and influence of jester and rumour.

Every one internally illumine Suryadeep and Nawab also influence of jester and satire. Every one had a hope of vigorous day.

So they were in discipline. They were subsequently seat in bus. So our bus stand at infront of main gate.

Our distination was no so long. After watched the real picture of main gate.

Our heart thrill with harmonise reboking.

The strong soldier in uniform was stand at infront of main gate in welldressed healthy soldier is ornament of western head command gate.

Remaining soldier's stand besides the main gate.

Even a civillian's walking at main gate.

Every one was great knight and warrior's in uniform that's a very pleasure experience for us our blood was prolific bestowed intended in Grace.

When we entred in main gate it was a today different experience no one could imagine. Every where disciplined men's and woman they were engaged in their work. That's why every where peace spreaded. Every thing was systematically stablished small unique tinny green grass park maintained under knight soldier's. No rush on the road under military governing every where sufficient man power on the military duty.

No one hang in the compulsion of argument. Every one lived for their goal. They focused for that with in chearfully attitude. They weared same uniform no one have expensive than another. No one feel inferior to their comred's in any way like civilians life.

They have same identity that's a national defender.

We observed many impactful national properties this experience is a influence of our higher education. Which we were did in practically western head command is consist in many part like.

Many service corps eg. A.M.C. Signal Engineer ASC. A.E.C. JAG. Militry form etc and combat eg. Infantry Armourd Artillary is established here that's a extremely proud of nation. We were watched every scenercis with our naked eye's we began to realy understood about Indian Military structure we were realy delighted because it's not our imagination its our real experience.

Every where green tale tree's surrounded the commands and it's situated on the foot hill's of Himalaya's and famous Chandi Devi temple is also. Occured here it's a very peacefull but disciplined atmospheric vally place. Which is governing under military government.

The command was well structured by training centre shooting range unique park and foreigners varieties of flowers officers mess, officer's banglow Jawan mess, and their residence golf course park for officer's sports ground, constracted expensive building and residence for V.I.P and higher Rank's officer's well planned jungle specially disigned for combat officers for their war planning and practise and western head command hospital with confluence of modern and specialist doctor's they always sacrifice for their's soldier's and officer's their service is unparallelled.

These all sceneries bringing and thrill us with new life styles that's totally different to the civilian's life today bird is unvisibly due to the modern life style of human being's. They spoil the forest and constructing the building in every metrocity.

Natural sceneris is eloped. But western head command of Indian Army is fully decorated by natural vagetition different varieties of trees and foreigner flowers.

So foreigner bird's and butterfly can not prevent their self to the effection of like a paradise natural vegetation, sceneries which is a proud of foot hills of Himalaya's so we visited these paradise atmosphare. We made eye glance at out side of window of our bus the bus was crossed these all beautiful sceneries and we all watches with carefully it was a totally different world's for as and basically for my other comrade's whose basicaly from civilian background. It's a time which provide them a correct knowledge of Indian militry because the story of Indian Army they litsen by any another person. But it's a time when they realy watches by their naked eyes.

Actually our camp was attached with I/IV Gorkha Rifles but in western head command many other Regiment and service courps settled. So we began to understand that it's a main head command of north western India. Which is dominante at whole north west of Indian Army we all of them in NCC uniform so our uniform realises as a combat officer, so we never fell that like a civilian's we determined for our target our vision was clear no compulsion. No excuse, no pain no mercy fully ready for combat officer's training. Finally our Bus was runing in green valley of Himalaya's which was captured for Indian military western head command. Foreigner bird's sated in park with consequently, their presence made Rainbow on the earth. It was beginning of winter season of north India.

The month of October so every polar regional siberian bird's came back to return from rusty north polar climate to subtropicual mansoon climate of Indian mother land the climate of indian mother land was moderate and so it's a very pleasant climate for every human being's of earth we were in jouney and very close to our destination that's why my every comreds had a respended eye and tryed to assume the whole knowledge of Indian militry structure and it's leadership quality and definatly we had a warm approval by defence government of India for our further training with I/IV Gorkha Rifles we wanted to became a Disciple of combat officer of Indian Army because for upcoming future. Which will be lead by as we did not learned by Indian Army for trust about fate we assumed only discipline idea wisdom and hard work create a leader.

We were in NCC uniform it's very different than civilian cloth's but uniform brought very attraction because it's fully decorated by medal Leniyard Baire Belt and boot. But these all thing is not a tenura for attraction, it's a swear for serve the nation. We were follow the rule of unity and discipline nation first and every thing which is required for combat officer.

Uniform brought us responsibility not only for our self for our country. We avaided the thing's of vanities and materialist we were very cautious for trivial thing because if civilian did the mistake it's may be but if we did it. It will be question mark in our sense of humour and our training which we assumed in NCC.

So we were close to our final destination. So this achievement is delighted our spirit.

It's a upcoming winter season of north India but sun shining on the peack of Himalayas and more shining in the western head command it made the diamond like shining on the natural vegetation of under command.

Chandigarh is situated in North Western part of country but in winter season rarely cloud becoming freezing and dark rarely fog dark dreezling and the sky is overcast with cloud even but all clouds have dispersed seartous. It has became shunny but whole year there was scanty rainfall it is surrounded by hilly states Himachal, but further it is also winter day's is brightness as comparatively U.P. and Bihar where a group of major people die in winter season due to the poverty problem and winter day is so dark plenty of fog frezing air. It's a clamity of nature but these state is more closer than tropic of equator so it should be more shining day's as a Chandigarh who have more distance to tropic of equator than U.P and Bihar. Climate direct effecting the human beings due to rough climate the people of U.P and Bihar anable to work in freezing winter season and opposite in hot summar day's and rainy mansoon day's, it's a ealamity of nature so they are unable to utilise their sense of humour and natural resources, that's why poverty problem increasing in these state's but the climate of Chandigarh is playing vital role for it's people development.

They are more healthy and concentrated for their work so it's a merit of weather in North western India.

We were realy enjoyed in the Journey of combat military bus.

It's our first but precious experience of our life.

We were realy such some more deserving cadet than other because they were really recruited handful cadet in that course.

We had a combat uniform it's more varies than realy N.CC uniform but it's not allowed at the repoting day in our attachement with 1/iv Gorkha Rifles we were realy in our truth and our real importance finally our juarny of Green combat militry bus in great valley of in foot hills of green Himalyas are no more.

We were crossed the varies regiment courps western head command of Army hospital shivalic golf course ground finally we were reached at our final distination were the acquired 1/IV Gorkha Rifles.

Because we were attached with them for our further training our driver puss brake and speed of bus was gradually stopped our bus was stand in a big ground surrounded by a strong wall at the wall every where tag the moto of Gorkha Rifles so it's a sufficient to understood as that these area is aquired by only Gorkha Rifles another Regiment could not interfere or march in that particular area. So fifty meter away in front of the Gorkha ground a big building constructed and twenty five meter away from the ground a Road devided the building and ground the road was well connected with main road of western head command gate so two Jawan ordered as for down from the bus and we began down from the bus. Further consequently we made a combat line according to our NCC rule and regulation the line shows our earlier training which we did in NCC. Then we were watched a JCO and a hawaldar came and warmly welcomed us for our further training. He was introduced himself that his name was NB/ Subedar Jagat Gurung. He was told that he is our master in our training and began to advice as about small and big particular of our final training and Residence with Gorkha Rifles. He watches as the building and told that a residence of Gorkha and we will stay with them in the building.

They will provide as a seprate bed, blanket, pillow and a moshquitonet. It was a month of October and very pleasure climate spread in whole north India, but moshquitonet was necessary for every Jawan and NCC cadet according to Indian military rule and regulation.

It was a time to 11.40 am he begin to convence as that building was constructed for Jawan and N.C.O not for J.C.O (NB/Subedar, Subedar, Subedar Major) and officer.

Officer stayed in officer enclave and J.C.O stayed in J.C.O enclave and he strickly advised that our movement in J.C.O and officer enclave is strickly prohibited we can stay in that particular building, we had no right for movement on the road or any where without permission of our master's he has convence as that in the building, the soldier was stayed in four separate groups.

1. Head Quarter
2. Delta
3. Charlie
4. Bravo

he was told that we will comprises in three different group, so our number, was

1. Yashpal Punchhi
2. Atul Kumar Pandey

3. Yatin Saroha
4. Suryadeep Singh
5. Jagdev Yadav
6. Nawab Khan
7. Chayan Chahal
8. Menan Anand
9. Brijesh Dhingra
10. Daljeet Singh Dahiya
11. Neelu Thakur
12. Sudu Rana
13. Sivendar Pandey
14. Komal
15. Vijay Singh Mehata
16. Santu Gupta

There are four group but the cadet of my college was shifted in remain these Quarter

1. Head Quarter
2. Delta
3. Charlie
4. Bravo

NB/Subedar Jagat Gurung was comprises as in three Quarter.

1. Charle–Atul Kumar Pandey, Jagdev Yadav and Nawab Khan

2. Delta–Yatin Saroha, Choudhary Suryadeep Singh Beniwal.

3. Remain Cadet and our senior under officer, Sivendar Pandey was shifted in headquarter.

After conversation of Jagat Gurung he was ordered as for consequently in line for attend the party in Gorkha Building which was organise for our warmly welcomed. Where they provided every healthy and hygiene lunch, consequently we take a haftey lunch because we were hunger we could not got our breakfast in the early morning. In the building ground attended.

A young Army officer, captain Koushal Anand who was our all over incharge in the camp and for our training. He was introduce himself to as he was very fit attractive and handsome his speech was very effective for every one that was allivated our moral so high he was uses very pure word.

We were impressed by him and his all activities after introduction caption was go away from building.

And we shifted in our different head quartor Actually every college of Chandigarh and Punjab university cadet participated in the camp, so their are so four head Quartor.

1. Charilie
2. Bravo
3. Head Quarter
4. Delta.

These all cadet shifted with as and some shifted in other head Quartor.

Atul, Jagdev, Nawab was shifted with in Charlie and our Quarter master was Adam Lepeha sir who was N.C.O. and our master of Quartor. So we got order by our master NB/ Subedar Jagat Gurung for rest to the 5 pm evening and every quartor had their own quarter master who suggest the cadet for discipline and combat officer life. They provided as a seprate three single bed for as we are very tiered and take a rest for 5 p.m. evening. Our room was very broad and their were two door devided to our room one sider in shifted the Jawan of Gorkhas and one side shifted NCC cadet.

Our mastar Adam Lepcha sir, was shifted with as he was hawaldar, but Knight warrior, he was masters in Khukhri war earlier he was posted in Jammu and Kashmir in as a Jawan but in a operation between Indian Army and terrorist Adam Lepcha sir was killed five terrorists by his own Khukuri that's why laterly he was became a N.C.O. Hawaldar. He was very charming person and desent tried to teach as every small and big particular of combat soldier and their life and sacrifice their sense of responsibility.

Yatin and Suryadeep shifted in Delta Quarter and my every comred's and (senior under officer Sivendar Pandey and Komal dweled in head quarter's Batalion.

In remain Bravo batalion in shifted the cadet of other college. Every cadet of varies college was become a confleuence with each other and shifted with each other acording to ordered of our master NB/*SUB* Jagat Gurung.

Every Quarter had their own a Quarter Master at the rank of N.C.O. and had a senior under officer, Rank was decided on the basis of seniority the S.U.O. of Charlie was Deepak Sharma who was from Khalsha College.

Delta had no any senior they connected with head quartor their S.U.O was Sivendar Pandey so acording to obey of NB/ Sub Jagat gurung we were on rest we were at II floor of building we had our separate Bed. Blanket and pillow we changed our NCC uniform and weared trouser and civilian sports uniform and waited for our 5. p.m. when we stand at at II floor The Natural picture of great Himalaya's was accquired our heart The scene was great green mountain, and high pick covered by snow. Snow peack looks like paradise of our earth. These paradise like mountain come under Himanchal Pradesh North west state of India. The peace of cant was emagine and it's a true example of Discipline and great structure of Indian military. In Civilian life if four people gathered at a place crowd and soundly voice suddenly spreading in whole atmosphere but in military cant thousand of men live with each other but they do not made noise without any reason and they are more happy and healthy than civilian when we seen our quarter master Adam Lepcha we were susprised because he was a knight and awarded by gallantry award he was earning less than a manager or a businessman. But he is more physically and psycologically fit than a good business man or Pvt. company manager his presence of mind was so good and he was treated us as a his child. He was very happy to our attachment with them our bed was consequently first at the began to door Jagdev Yadav than my bed Atul

Kumar Pandey and in last Nawab Khan, than stayed the cadet of other college the cadet of other college our heart was very delighted to the experience and it's a frist day's of our traening so we were very ambitious to knowing about what will happen at when we will assemble at the 5 pm in roll call parade in evening what they will announced for our further training. The begining of combat military training was started it's our first day's but we had lot's of hope to this precious camp. After rest of 4.20 p.m. Adam Lepha Sir loudly ordered as for wakeup and Nimbly we wake up and get ready for roll call pared we are in three cadet from D.A.V. college Nawab, Atul, and Jagdev Yadav and other cadet was also stayed with as but they are from different colleges.

So we take care to each other to concentrate for our training because every cadet had most important for every college because a single cadet could win a medal for their college that's why every one playing vital role and in our group Atul was good Atheltes so every one having a hope to myself in atheletes in my college. So after toilet fresh we were Nimble for Roll call parade. Which was a type of Assembly where every senior Army officer assembled regard's the announced the every angle of training and our daily routine and which thing is suitable and not suitable for our further training.

And the rule and regulation of Indian Army and which allowed for NCC Cadet. So according to ordered of NB/ Subedar Jagat Garung at the right time 5 p.m in evening we assemble in building for role call pared where two hawaldar and NB/Sub Jagat Gurung presented we consequently in line laterly a jipsy came with red light on top of gipsy with syren it made the silent atmoshphor because it was captain Koushal Anand when he was down from jypsy every Jawan Hawalder and NB/Subedar, Jagat Gurung concentrating and proudy saluted him he was came with style and looked like a hero because he was young and had more importance than all other Jawan and J.C.O gradually he was came with close as and asked our situation and every suply which is provided by Indian Army he was told us that we will suffer to water supply problem full food supply may be many difficulties come in our training because it's everything is part of our militry training he was convence as that do not loss your confidence wherenever you will be hanging in the problem because you are attach with Gorkha for what for learn the life style and combat training of Indian Army and Gorkha. So it's not so easy it's a great task so for learn these all thing number of difficulties come in your training period so in these period, so do not blame to any one that is responsible for your tough training you should realise to your self that is you are main responsible for this tough training because these all difficulties come in every combat officer's life and after pass in these all exam one could became a leader of combat military of Indian Army. So do not fear to these all difficulties make strong to your self that's all strong difficulties.

When captain finished his speech then started fire in cigarate and began smoke in his style his was cigarate smoking assume when he uses his first fog consantratly seen as who is sluggiss cadet once he find a cadet who was not active ordered him that began push up till the end of his cigrate his it's line became very famous in under every cadet. So we learned and entertainment by him.

So after speech and a cigrate captain was go away and NB/Subedar Jagat Gurung started his speech than Hawaldar started their speech. In these all speech finish our hours 5. p.m. to 7 p.m. in evening and within two hour's we were do not made movement in our body because we all ready learned by them momvement or any activities in roll call pared is against to the military rule and regulation so we do not made any bad activities so after speech NB/Subedar Jagat Gurang ordered as for take the dinner than sleep in before 9.30 o clock in evening. After Roll call pared we were entered in mess that was our first experience in military mess that mess were run for Jawan and N.C.O. not for J.C.O. and officer so NCC cadet was also attached with the Jawan mess.

Their are four mess I mean every Quartor had their spreate mess we were take dinner in Charlie mess. The quality of food was so good everage but not in the favour of NCC cadet because that mess was run for Gorkha Jawan that's why they prepared food in the favour of Gorkhas Jawan that night they provide.

Chapati, potato mix vegetable and milk made rice.

After dinner we could not walk in the varandaw are any where that was strickly prohibited so we moved for our Quarter in the Charlie we feel that after arrival at Gorkha rifles our touch with our other comred's was breack because they stayed with their own different Quartor. So Nawab Atul and Jagdev Yadav sleep in Charlie. That night was so pleasure before sleep Adam Lepcha Sir advise as that we have to need wake up in 3 am in morning because their are single bathroom and the water supply will be reduce after 3.30 o' clock and the reporting time was in pared ground was 4 am so we switch off at the 10 p.m. in night. We drooned in sleep than when some one puss as and cryed that wake up. I was wake up it was 3.10 a.m. after in consiousness. Adam Lepcha Sir advice as for it's our training so we could not got plenty of water he was told as that their are sufficient water in cant but they could not provide, because it's a part of our camp so nimbly we moved at bathroom where only one buke (Jug) water was available for a single cadet and every activities we need complete in a jug water because after that a drop of water was not available for as, so I complete poety and clean the anus, after that I made hand wash in the a Jug water, after utilize these activities I have half jug of water so taked brush and clean save with in only a jug water.

The amount of water was sufficient for sip a cadet but we finished our every activities in a single jug water.

It's a memories that I used a water in tuth brush clean save and in fash wash which water that was I used in after poety anus wash and in my latine Room. That time I realise a importance of water in civilian life we daily wastes many fresh water. That was our training we suffered to the water problem but we learned many usefull thing of life that civilian can not imazine it was our first task of our training we finished our activities with nimbly but time was became 4. am o clock so suddenly we wear sport's cloth's and as reported at pared ground.

Where our N.C.O Athelets was waited every one reported at the right time and consequently stand in line our NB/SUB was attend as and ordered as, for five kilometer of running we began to running of 5 km. with our Athelets N.CO their were 110 cadet from various colleges but I was come under five cadet in running in first days I was secure III position in 110 cadet that was great beginning of D.A.V college sector 10 D. My comred's of D.A.V became glad for my achievement's they have a answer for our senior which they were made comments against as but our determination and hard work made them false and secured a postion in western head command Chandimandir Chandigarh.

My achievement bring them confidence for final competition with in varies college of Chandigarh.

After five km of running we retrun at Gorkha pared ground where we did every exercise to till the 6.30 am o clock after 6:30 o clock we became tired but we did not have right a for rest come back to return in the Gorkha building and take tea break at 7. a.m. after tea break they provide as 15 minutes of time for changed the uniform than come to back to return in Gorkha ground. We changed and come back to return. Where we consequently stand in line and NB/Jagat Gurung teaches as that about weapon's room, he was told that mobile and camera was not allowed where and we never discused about these experience to any civilian after that we entered in weapon room we were shocked where every weapon of indian Army was available, Insas L.M.G A.K. 47, carbine 84 m.m. Rocket lancher, he was introduced as to every single weapon and he was told that we will train in weapon riding first time we come in weapon room but every small and big weapon touched and catch and try to take if in our hand he was told that their are many weapon so we can not be a master in one day in all.

We have to need sacrifice for every day for a single weapon daily it's compulsory for as.

Than we take a insas L.M.G. and according to NB/subedar we moved at pared ground for our weapon training their we assumble specialist in weapon and tryed to teach as in pared ground we comprises in four part. Every group have a specialist in INSAS L.M.G and they tryed to teach as about small thing weak and strong point of L.M.G and how to we could ride and every thing. They were teach us about Insas L.M.G is indian manufactured weapon it was made in ishapur west bengal and this weapon is very famous in Indian Army and other Armed forces because soldier easily could target in any position like if you are standing and enemy suddenly attack on your self so easily you can target him in standing position if you are sitting and enemy made target you can shoot him in sitting position, lining position and every position that's why this weapon is very famous but A.K. 47 and Rocket launcher have their own different specility like you can not shoot any one to in every position.

They have their different style like Rocket launcher is specially prepared for tank attack it enemy crossed the Line of control you can fire Rocket launcher at corner of tank they will be destroyed and other carbine uses in different position so it was time to finish the weapon training watch was beeping at the 11 am o' clock so its a our breakfast time our N.C.O ordered as for join a line in consequently we follow his order and join it and followed his obey and reach in mess for our morning break fast we finished our break at the 11.40 o' clock because when entered in room we waited because all ready Gorkha Jawan was on line for morning breakfast so we take the time. So after break fast the reporting in parade ground was necessary. So we reported in pared ground for our further training in education. They educated as in military science.

The class was run by Education Hawaldar they teach as about classification of Indian military what is service corp's and what is combat Army and what types of different it in. How they serve for nation they teach as about the main combat Army is Infantry 2-artilary and 3-Armourd. These three are part of combat Army and only these are participated in war otherwise other service corps are only supported them in war as well as in peace but only these there are playing vital role in Indian Army. Its not mean other service corps having less important than combat its not trees service corps is also playing a vital role in supporting Army like medical corps handle the patient of Indian Army. If some one injured by bullet that time only doctors and nurses handle them and treat them with carefully so like it. The work of engineering corps is the destroye the way of enemy and maintain the every maferial thing of Indian Army and construct the building. These are the classification of Indian military organisation.

Infantry is also comprises in many part like 1-Light Infantry 2. Machanise Infantry B. and different type of they are direct handle enemy to in the war time that's why infantry mean. The man power of Indian Army who tackle battle in on foot by their machine gun and Khukure or their by physical and pshycological power and India is surounded by hilly region and every dangerious and sensetive border come under mountain so in these condition the importance of infantry is so high and they take havy risk in war time.

Artillery: The Importance of Artillery is also most important in war time because they are destruct the enemy by tank but these tank's is anabale to climbing on top of mountain it's also a part of combat Army.

Armourd: They are attack on enemy by bomb and rocket launcher by small tank they can their climb their tank on hill but they are enable to climbing top of mountain that's why they are also playing a vital role in war time it is also a part of combat Army.

So one thing I want to clear that the chief of Army staft only selected in combat Army. Other service, corps are a have no right to send their officer for chief of Army staff that's why the importance of infantry is so high compratively other services corp's it should be because they are direct participated in ugly war and finish it by their unmatchable type of sense of honour's. The class was very interesting it was 1.30 p.m. so it's a time for lunch our N.C.O. orderd us for lunch and we consequently in the line by with pared entered in mess and take the meal after launch the time was goining on 2 p.m. o clock so after lunch by order of N.C.O. we reported at pared ground and did practise for dreal I was good in studies, sport's, and every ectivities but not good in dreal but tryed improved it with in one hour of tough practise we became very tired because we wake up at 3:10 a.m. and it was going on 3 p.m. it's totaly struggle of 12 hour's so lastly at 3 p.m. our N.C.O. order as for one hour of rest at 3 p.m. to 4 p.m. but Hawalder Neeraj Thapa order us for report at 4 p.m. in the parade ground's regard's evening sport's that game was decided by officer Captain Koushal Anand so by his obey we follow and came back to return at gorkha building at 3.15 p.m o clock at the arrival at our quartor we feel like come from a war we were very tiered and changed the uniform and did not wanted to waste the time and take bed rest of near about 30 to 45 minute because at 4 p.m. our arrival at gorkha ground was necessary. So take a deeply rest realy I want to say's my experience that was really rest because full days we struggle by both side by physically and by maintainly that's a realy enjoy of life, it's different thing we had only 45 minute but we really that rest being in our body deeply pleassure that type of joy only can feel a realy former or real soldier suddenly the watch was beeping I wake up and seen that the time was 3.45. so I awaked with my two other comred's Nawab and Jagdev for evening game we prepared for evening game. We prepared and by timely reported at pared ground. Where captain Koushal was all ready reported who was announce that the today was cadet plays the match of foobtall it will be happen between Gorkha Jawan and NCC cadet who was announce if cadet win the match they will take meal in officer mess till the end of their training we became very delighted. Because we were all irritated to Jawan mess.

So warmly we began to plays the match between gorkha we choosed good defend and good player varies college of Chandigarh. I was also became a part of football match we tried to threat the Gorkha we did full hard work. Uses a belter goal kipper but could not stop our loss in the match Gorkha was professional player. There were many player in Gorkha's team playing for national team but many players in our team who first time playing the foot ball match we lost the football match. But fully enjoyed in because we fully sacrifies to ourself for football match that's why we were not realise for our defeat the match was continued at 4 p.m. To till the 6 p.m. After football match we were very tiered and Really we wanted to take rest but NB/Sub. Jagat Gurung told that you did hardwork but it's a untiring hard work because you are a upcoming soldier so you should be determined loyal hardworker and do not feel pain because pain is temperary but Pride is foreever so live for pride and forget the bluddy pain. I am here Army medical corps will be fell down on the earth we will climb you. So do not think about your self think about your nation. After his speech was influence of Patriotic full of motion responsiblity. We bring our soul to in consiouness and and pain was suddenly fell down NB/SUB Jagat ordered us for you have 10 minute of time go in your room.

Changed sport's dress and wear uniform than report at Gorkha building ground for further roll call parade go with fast. After finish his word we ran away from the ground and did that what he told than reported at the right time in Gorkha building ground so that evening captain Koushal Anand was came in his personal Wagonar car and down with in style from his car and asked our situation and earlier before one day's of experience in the camp he was asked how much cadet have problem and for what many hand stand they have complain of morning water problem and electricity problem and other complain he listen every thing with careful of every cadet than replied gentleman you will have suffered to these all problems to till the end of your camp because it's all problem is a part of your training. Finally he asked a comic question how much cadet have suffered to the problem of connectivity with his girl friend so many hand stand. I have no any problem because I was single that time so he ordered the J.C.O. and Jawan for provide 20 minute us calling for our parents and girl friend he was commited that he will be provide delectricity within 2 hours for mobile charging and then he goes away from Gorkha building ground. It was at 8 p.m of evening totally we stand two hour's in Gorkha building ground. Than we moved for our dinner that night was also prepared chapati mix veg and milk made rice (Khir) Khir was very tasty so I was told Jagdev Yadav to beg the Kheer but according to rule we finished our meal But our interest was in milk made ricese him so Jagdev Yadav was small height and funny person he was began to dancing in mess so every jawan was laughing about him he keeps plate on his head and made dancing so they asked him what he want he replied that his desire is milk made rice (Kheer) so with in cheerfully attitude his bring the plate we querrel on one plate. I made largely he comedy abused us me and Nawab but we were very happy with each other. and after dinner we moved on Charlie house. Before camp our imagination was turn into realism we crosses our day's in camp with very cheerfully and secured good mark in every compitition like in dreal. Yashpal Punchhi, Atheletis, Atul Kumar Pandey, we remembered how our senior insulted us, and made comments against our performance in the camp, every thing was comfortable but our senior and Senior under officer of Head Quarter Sivendar Pandey was suffer to miss understanding between their junior mean our coursemate and he always reported at late in morning for running so NB/ Subedar Jagat Gurung many time insulted him infront of every cadet but he don't improve his self one night he was came in my room and suddenly started crying and bringing tear in his eyes. I was asked him, Sir what happen why you are sainty so he was told that Pandey your coursemate abused me, and they do not follow my command. I collect them and asked that what happen. They replied that Pandey Sir, always Ribuked us without any mistakes. They behave like innocence so I, Suryadeep and Jagdev convence them and strickly advised that don't commit again these type of rediculus activities and I convince them and unit remembered them the final competition between various colleges of Chandigarh. That is very importan for us. Nawab convince them if some one made rediculus activities and if we could not win medal in the camp so how you all of you can make eye glance with your senior. Who recognise himself and realise us that they are best. I told them medal is different thing but Pandey Sir is your senior and you should be respect for him.

Do not querrell with him and obey the rule and command of him. and do not forget this opportunity you were got after suffer the lot's of problem you have chance for proof your self so you should be full sacrifice for that if you will win the medal that's fine, but if you will unfortunately lost.

You will do not have a excuse and realise, so forget and determined for why you came for what, first you should understand if every cadet give their full of sacrifice and determination. We will well perform in the match after two days.

The final competition of shooting will be organise is already after two days with insas L.M.G. with real bullet so do not dispointed to your target consantrate to all of you because every cadet should consantrate for the final competition. You have a golden opportunity so every one comited for their full of job, and realy they are determination for final competition, but the problem was created between them because Sivendar

Pandey Sir 4 time SSB out that time so, he was fell down in under dipression so if any cadet made a joke he became serious about them that's why the problem was created between them and the distance between Charlei to Head Quarter was not so, less, so we had no sufficient time for, convence them.

Because whenever we will I mean Nawab, Jagdev and Atul was very comedian comic so every one like us and three cadet stayed with each other but further it is also after conversation they were totally changed and acclimatise to their self according to military rules and regulations.

So our routine was totally set and we almost prepare for final competition. They keep quite all off to every quarrel activitie with each other and final competition is one day's more so we focused for that. Before Army attachement. I had no experience in the shooting but our trainer in Army attachement camp majestically trained us in Insas L.M.G. and the competition will be in shooting with Insas L.M.G. so I was and my comred's had no any hope to me in shooting. They have only hope to me in atheletes. But Chowdhary Suryadeep Singh Beniwal was good shooter with .22 gun.

So he won many medal in varies competition before Army Attachement camp in shooting so we had full confidence him for final victory in shooting.

Chawdhary Suryadeep was good practised in shooting and he was many time made a victory in shooting competition. That's why, we were in stress free about in shooting. He was also with in confidence but it's his first experience in the Army attachement if he will weldon peform in upcoming competition. We had a trust that if he will do not win a final medal that's don't worry but he will select in top five cadet in shooting. It will be also a big achievement.

Finally came a day's of most jubilition which was a day of a final competition of shooting with Insas L.M.G. like other days. We were followed the every task from early morning to noon after a lunch we assumblee in parade ground where our master NB/Subedar Jagat Gurang Sir was attended and announced that today's organise a final competition of shooting which will be held in shooting ground of western head command Chandigarh. Actually Western head command had only a merely shooting ground and western head command mean a capital of western region of military so their are so many regiment and corp's is all ready stayed in the command and at every time any one regiment practised that's why their were merely a time when shooting ground was free from bullet.

So the time was decide of 2 p.m. earlier. It was 12 p.m. but Madras regiment was practised that's why our captain Koushal Anand postponded the time 12 pm to 2 pm so the competition was held between varies college of Chandigarh. Every cadet had a opportunity for became a hero in shooting. Their were no restriction between cast cride and religion everyone had same opportunity same training and same target. There were no any reservation.

Policy like civilion life every one was fully librated for heat the bullet on target.

So according to order of NB/Subedar Jagat Gurang we were consequently hanged a gun of Insas L.M.G. on shoulder and stand in line our N.C.O. provided us a jungle helmet safty for our head by bullet they provided us a green colour of military truck.

That was a juarny of upcoming combat military officer. We were in discipline and reminded every thing what we were learned about this gun because our N.C.O. Neeraj Thapa Sir fully trained us in Insas L.M.G. so we were in a jurney of military green colour of truck with a hope of new achievement every one was extemely delighted because they will got the opportunity of real gun to shoot the real bullet that was only possible for a soldier of Indian Army.

But really we were had some extra ordinary power for this wonderful opportunity so we wanted to did full sacrifice for that competition, our bus was running and we made a loudly patriotic song. With our N.C.O. of Gorkha, they were very delighted within our company.

So our journey with combat military truck was run for shooting ground. The truck was crossed a jungle where every trees and flower consquently stablished so I asked to N.C.O. about this forest who was told me that this jungle is specially designed for combat military training, and every young officer's and jawan practised for target against terrorist and he was told me that after shooting competition with in two day's will practise in the forest for learn about how we can shoot terrorist at the mountain sourrounding area and forest in J & K and Assam and he was told me that first I need to concentrate on today shooting competition so our combat military truck was crosses the whole forest and peace area of western head command of Chandimandir.

The combat bus was run for its final destination that was shooting ground we were very delighted for our imagine and gallent days.

So with in few hour's the bus was stoped our driver push the break to his leg and suddenly bus gradually stopped.

So after the order of our N.C.O we down from combat truck and that was shooting ground the scene of shooting ground was Assume no sound politly solylock before our arrival already our captain Koushal Anand our N.C.O and a Medical officer. Doctor captain Suraj Singh was presented.

Where assumbled many cadet from various colleges of Chandigarh in the hope of new best shooter of Chandigarh.

After our arrival we consequently stand in the line for gun shooting we seen in the ground was fully Solylock and they have made a statue of Duplicate terrorist in shooting ground firstly they announce that their are fifteen bullet in the gun and for best shootar you should be hit the target of terrorist chest and Head. The mark was consist on the many part max number secure at the heat of chest and head they were told that for best shootar cadet should be heat the more than 9 bullet on Right target. So according to our Quater company and five cadet was shooted with in one line with each other and fortunately D.A.V. was choosen for first, in the first line for shooting down.

1. Yashpal Punchhi
2. Jagdev Yadav
3. Atul Kumar Pandey
4. Daljeet Singh Dahiya
5. Nawab Khan

So we bend and keep's the gun Insas L.M.G. our a comred's of D.A.V pray's to god for our best perfcrmance in the shooting for our safety before fireing Captain Koushal Anand and N.C.O. mentain and improve our position for our firing and where assambale A.M.C. Doctor captain Suraj for if some thing happen wrong mean if some cadet injured in the firing they will admited them in western head command hospital Chandigarh so after right position we began firing to bullet we catches gun with our style and what we studies in fifteen day's of our training with Gorkha. They well trained us and we shooted with in firing our tear's suddenly fell down to our eyes because the effect of bullet we feel like burn our eyes and the sound of gun was very soundly to the noise of gun bird suddenly flying in the sky. So after continued firing with insas L.M.G. finally come a time to known the score of every single cadet secure score of my Comred is follow performance.

1. Nawab Khan ⟶ Poor
2. Jagdev Yadav ⟶ Not satisfied
3. Yashpal Punchhi ⟶ Good performance
4. Daljeet Singh Dahiya ⟶ Poor performance
5. Atul Kumar Pandey ⟶ Best Shooter

So after our group every one followed it merely a cadet crosses the score of 8 so every cadet of varies college from Chandigarh was participated in shooting. Infact best shooter with .22 gun Suryadeep Baniwal but they could not secure good mark and in last three cadet of my college was became best shooter Komal, Sir who was our senior in NCC and lastly recruited for officer's (O.T.A.) my comred's Yatin Saroha, lastly recruited in I.T.B.P. as a S.I. and Atul Kumar Pandey. So their were five college of Chandigarh but only six cadet was became best shooter in Chandigarh but in all six will be final compition Announce for final competition, who will secure large number they will be got gold medal in shooting but our captain Koushal Anand was told that these all are best shootar and they deserves for medal, so final competition was decide that day after tomorrow so shooting competition, so first day's shooting competition was over.

So after shooting competition the shining day's was converted into dark night so we urgest in truck and a imgine journey of combat military truck to Gorkha building. That was nice experience so after arrival at Gorkha building, we attended. Roll call parade where our captain Koushal sir was announced that next day decided for combat jungle training he continued his speech that jungle training is most important for infantry officer because in border areas where militant hiden for terrorist attack in the country so this type of training is very useful for their incounter and fully destroy to their Aim so we concentrated and waited for next day's because it was a Ambition that we wanted to know's that how a combat officer's searched the militant in jungle (forest) and how their team worked so after roll call parrade we were moved for dinner in charile mess where we got, non-veg. and became very glad because after tough exercise we were hungry and when we got a meal in dinner that was a paradise experience. After of hafty dinner we moved for our Charlie Quarter and before 10 p.m. we switched off.

So like every day's we followed that's all exercise participated in every activities but our training was no more tough like other earlier days because our training was four days more, that night was decided for jungle training another days was final shooting competition and than physical running,

Rope climbing. It was decided in one days. So in the ground our N.C.O. teaches us some Gorkha's word that the moto of Gorkhas was Kapar Hunda Bhandu Myrnu, Ramro, mean it's better to die than be a coward, and another moto was, one bullet and one enemy we all very inspired to these two moto and it's a real that we did very tough training but we feel it's a way which can change our life style we feel that our body movement was totally changed. Who was very sluggish in our company becaming a full of spirit and a panther like nimblty.

It's a impact of training with Gorkha's.

Once, that evening in Roll call pared our captain Koushal Anand was attended and made very politily behave to us told that it I know's every cadet suffer to tough exercise but you should be feel proud to yourself because your attachment with Gorkha's will provide you a new life style you will be a leader of society. It is not compulsary you all of you become a part of Indian, Army but it's compulsry where you join you will change the orgnisation with influence of loyalty honesty determination, and you will do your work with fairly and always remembered that you are a part of Indian Army, because you are a cadet for life time at the end of his speech he was told that after dinner, we will join the company for jungle training in the night so after speech he was gone away than we moved for dinner that night Gorkha's prepared a mix veg milk made rice and and chapati. The quality of food was not equally as well as domestic dinner but we became habitual for these meal. After dinner we reported in pared ground, where our mastar's was NB/SUB Kartikeyan in Army education courps, and N.C.O. Neeraj Thapa and C.H.M. Adam Lepcha these all are our instructor for jungle training. They choosed NB/SUB A.E.C. for map reading and compas training and N.C.O. for our weapon taining and how we can take position and handle the gun in a danger forest because where every terrorist is also well trained for fight to any Army so minor careless may be very blunder mistake so at this topic they teaches us about jungle training before enetered in dark jungle we should be wear jungle cloth and made our voice like any animal or bird who stayed in jungle.

Because if we will follow this type of activities terrorist easily could not understood about our movement in jungle so they trained us to speak like bird and animal and further it is also they suggest us that we should be known, which animal and bird wake up in the evening because if we make a voice like any animal who is sleeping in the evening so enemy could understood, about us. After that all we understand that we command to our comrade's in the voice of animal and bird. So it's a journey of a combat officer it's a training which provided us a knowledge of how we can serve our motherland to external enemy and force. and we appreciate about training with Indian Army of Gorkha Rifles so we entered in jungle for our training and after advise their were very minor condition when any one could mistake so we take a gun in our hand with position and really we feel that's a operation in somewhere in Jammu and Kashmir or Assam. Where after commission seventy percent young infantry Army officer, posted so we continued movement in jungle till the 2 am under command. NB/SUB Kartikuyan A.E.C. and our some warrior's N.C.O. like Neeraj Thapa and Adam Lepcha and with in five hours of training every one was serious about their training they do not made any unrecognised voice. The experience was super so besides the jungle their were situated a Army officer's mess where every officers celebrated the party their wives was half nude, and closely dancing with another officer not her husband and drunked alcohal and their husband feel comfortable they also changed a woman and dancing with another woman and they smooch with each other in western style. That was uncomfortable we feel that they were not serious about their life partner but we enjoyged to a meal away by only watch the scene and our training was so good physically. We became tired but mentally we were enjoyed the scene of officer's mess. Where their many laxury expensive car's parked and every officer enjoyed that night that a life of royalty but our NB/SUB and N.C.O. worked hard with us so I feel guilty in favour of J.C.O. and Jawan, and other hand because my father was also a J.C.O.

In officer mess J.C.O. and Jawan of Indian Army do not have to right for entry they could not enjoyed their self to like a officer our J.C.O. was M.A. pass but whole night he was bussy with us in his duty but every officer's with in expensive civilian cloth's enjoyed the life of royalty they were changed the woman and whole night they danced with wines and wives of their comrade's, their comrades did not had any objection. So at 3 O' clock by order NB/SUB Our training was over of Jungle training and we moved for our Gorkha building we arrived at Gorkha building and Nawab Jagdev and me moved for our Charlie Quarter.

We entered in room with our master's Adam Lepcha sir. And 3 O' clock we switched off. Next days we wake up at 8 O' clock mean three and half hour's late but we followed that's all activities what we did daily.

And that was a day of final competition of shooting only six was best shooter and that was a day of gold medal in shooting. My comrades had a extremely hope to myself.

So till the noon we all six shooter follow the all exercise with every cadet but 2 O' clock was decided for our final shooting competition but Punjab regiment was busy on shooting ground, shooting was postponded to 5 O' clock in evening so at 4.30 O' clock we weared our NCC uniform, only six cadet from 110 cadet and remain was participated in daily games so we sit in combat military truck for our final gold medal everyone had a heart bit but I was sure about my training because in training Neeraj Thapa sir was fully trained us and with interest I was followed that's all so I had remembered that sight elitement and sight eye we should between inch so with green combat military truck our journey was finished our driver. Puss the brake and truck gradually stopped so after our arrival in shooting ground. The ground was not free.

Punjab regiment was bussy in shooting and we reported at the right time 5 O' clock in the evening but till the 8 O' clock. Punjab regiment was busy in shooting.

They librated shooting ground at 6.30 p.m that time a shining Noon turned into evening.

So that was not a properly good time for our shooting with Insas L.M.G. so we complain to our captain Koushal Anand Sir because in dark night how it may be possible that we can watch our target but captain sir was told that Gentlemen you all of you good shooter but their are a merely a shooting ground. So alway's it will be busy with any another regiment so do not think about medal just hit the target and follow the training rule if you have any problem so we do not provide a medal to any one because it's not a healthy or fair competition.

Because we knows that in dark night how it may be possible that any one could hit the target and you have only two day's more of your final training so today you have to need complete it so we take position and keep Insas L.M.G. and hit the target we had ten bullet and in position any one could not watch their target so in Air we fire to bullet so we did fire ten bullets my one bullet hit the Yatin target but after a fire N.C.O. Checked every target did not had hit by any one but Yatin was hit besides me so his target I was hit in unconciousness. So after result with in six cadets they did not hit any target. So captain was unable to announced the final result of winner because really no one was winner but my bullet only hit the target but target was not set for my self that was for Yatin. So captain sir asked to me Pandey if the medal goes in Yatin side that's mean finally D.A.V. will be winner in shooting so I know's you shoot the target but that was Yatin target so if you have objection I will do not provide medal to any one but if you have do not any problem so according to rule I will provide to Yatin so you can think. I was told that night sir I have do not any problem. You provide medal to Yatin every one have problem they told me Mr. Pandey you are shooted the target so how will Yatin got the medal but we have in majority because D.A.V have three best shooter but other college merely have a single or come or nil so I was convince to Komal sir because he was also best shooter (laterly who was became Army officer's) that we should be concentrate on college medal not our self who was glad did not had any objection so finally captain Koushal Anand was announced that these all six are best shooter with in Insas L.M.G. but Yatin Saroha was won the medal but finally who was told that Mr. Atul Kumar Pandey is also best shooter who was looked me and pass smile.

My every commred became essentric to the win of medal in shooting because Their were only two competition one is all over best performance for three people but medal was provide only for one and another is shooting competition. Our senior was defeated to our achievement before camp I was committed for best performance and we did it. Finnally that was our day's Sivendar Pandey Sir made a call to Mayank sir, and told that's our achievement they socked and he was told that Mr. Atul Pandey is best shooter here.

It's our win to our senior thought. Their were many best shooter but finally Yatin Saroha became a winner with in all five. The best shooter was not Brahman or Kshatriya who was from seheduled caste so according to government of India he could not win the any medal because who from seheduled caste but who defeated many Kshtriya. I was only Brahman with in six. Who win without any reservation policy but it was happen and I am witness of his final victory may be in dark night come one other cadet heat his target it's different thing but we six cadet are best shooter in all 110 cadet in various colleges of Chandigarh but why government follow the policy of reservation. I do not knows. It's my opinion they should be provide them economically support but not in competition it's only a way of collection the vote, it's totally wrong in favour of our society classification. So next days was our final competition, so after shooting we moved in Gorkha building our comred's hang us on their head. We moved for our dinner than switched off at 10 pm so wake at the right time today's is final comptition in dreal and physical.

First begin in running it was began at 4.30 a.m. their were 110 cadets and I secure second position in Athelets and first position was a cadet from government college in long jump. I secure first position at the rope climbing I could not climbing so their were became final list of physically training and in dreal (Yashpal Punchhi from D.A.V. to secure first position (Laterly who moved for canada for his L.L.M.) But I could not secure good position in dreal. So every thing was completed at evening 4 p.m. so in every one waited for their name it will be announced by captain Koushal Anand in Roll call pared. So our NB/SUB Jagat Gurang order us for hour's of game. So we began game 4.30 to 5.30 than we were assemble for Roll call parade. Where captain Koushal Anand was attended who announced the name, first–best shooter.

1. Yatin Saroha—D.A.V. 10 — Best Cadet in drill

2. Yashpal Punchhi–D.A.V. 10 D — Best physical training.

3. Jack from—Government college — Best cadet in all over performance.

4. Atul Kumar Pandey–D.A.V. 10 D.A.V. was became a winner and joining and crazy to their cadet after our achievement the news of our achievement spread in whole college by Sivendar Pandey. We had one day's more in western head command Chandimandir Chandigarh.

We made a mile stone with in ten year's D.A.V have a best performance that was our day's 'A' days of achievement which we got by very hard work determination sacrifice and unity.

We defeated our senior to our unparallel approach on our work and duty.

It's a achievement of ambition wisdom and hard work. But our achievement was not a achievement of a single cadet it's a achievement of our team our comrade's and our thought that's we all committed before the camp that we can do it and really we did it.

So after Roll call pared we moved for our dinner that's night Gorkha's prepared the non veg. It's very testy meal. After dinner we moved for our Charlie, Quarter that night I was very glad and sleep with Nawab Khan and I stuck with Nawab and Jagdev. Suddenly Adam Lepcha sir, was seen my activities, so their were no authorise that three cadets can sleep with each other but we became winner that's why we were glad and talk to each other Adam sir was seen and known Nawab was in his bed but I was away from my bed. So he was punish me that by sub my body and touch the door I did with cheerfully every one lough about my activities so after punishment, Adam Lepcha sir became emotional, he was told that you all cadet move day after tomorrow so I feel that you all of you like my small kid's. I convince him and promised for meet forever in the life as a their kids with in camp duration we had heartly attachment with them. So at the 10 p.m. we swiched off and that was a very pleasure night because next days was last day's in the attache with Gorkha so according to every day's we wake up in early morning and completed the running of five kilometer with captain Koushal Anand it's first time when captain sir was run with us.

After that is we completed break fast and assamble in gorkha Auditorium for medal contribution and litsen for the speech of colonel N.S. Rana who was commanding officer's of Gorkha Rifles.

So first captain Koushal Anand was came in the fully military uniform and decorated uniform with lot's of medal that was he won in the operation the medal was a symbol of glorry. So after that's captain Koushal was began to his speech and told that gentlemen you are a attache with Gorkha first defender of country so till the end of life you are a part of Gorkha's so never do the work wrong. And many meaningfull speech with in his speech. The commanding officer's of

Gorkha's colonel Rana was reported when his car entered in Gorkha building suddenly captain Koushal Anand J.C.O. Jagat Gurang fastly gone away from A the Gorkha Auditorium and warmly welcomed him. They saluted with activity to coloned N.S. Rana. First saluted captain Koushal Anand and NB/ Subedar Jagat Gurang than C.O. Rana, accepted and he was also saluted them it's a rule of Indian Army where every junior is saluting to their senior so colonel N.S. Rana entered in Gorkha Auditorium where we were assumbled we stand to our sit and wishes him that good morning sir, he was also accepted our proposal.

So he continued his speech that's gentlemen I hope you all of you want to be a officer's in Indian Army that's a fantastic thought. Like are became a very responsible in very early age so your desire is not uncomplete because you all ready attach with Gorkha Rifles where you learn how a real infantry soldier adjusting their life in every condition. Like they have no meaning of hot climate of Thar desert of Rajasthan or Sahara desert or minus temperature of Siachin in each and every condition they are fully ready for their duty without any excuse and you all of you earlier twenty day's learned the some condition of their life because you all faces the electricity problem water supply problem and who had suffered more problem those are glutton because we were provided you not sufficient food because that's all are a part of your training and really I am appreciate about your burning desire that no one cadet was drop out between in the training 110 cadet selected from varies college of Chandigarh and today these all are completed their tough training and further it is also I am realy appreciate to D.A.V. 10 D cadet they are more deserving in every competition they made a new history in this premier institution like best shooter Yatin from D.A.V. best dreal Yaspal Punchi and one of the most that all over in best performance goes for cadet Atul Kumar Pandey these all are focussed on their duty that's good and you all of you from Varies college of (U.T.) did well and he continued his speech that's gentlemen today is your last day's in Gorkha building because tomorrow we will send you in your college so I want to appeal to all of you that's if you had any problem with in camp so do not make camplain to any civilian because we heartly trained you as a our small kid's gentlemen India is no more rich than U.S. and U.K. and you are realy close to Army so if you miss using the thing so pouerty will be increase to day by day that's why we trained you that's judicious use of the money because money comes not easy so alway's respect it. And really you can understand the country's poverty problem you all really trained that's a jawan with in the war could leave their gun in any condition why because the cost of a gun is more expensive so how we could urgest it so and our country is poor we can not provide bulletproof jacket to every jawan J.C.O. and officer's and due to insufficient budget of defence government our many Jawan became martyr in comman operation so you are country's upcoming generation and country today depend on your thought so always utilise the money in good work do not involve in the whoring, gambling and drinking always judicious use of the money and you all of you totally difference than other you are more responsible than other civilian so you should guide them for your nation building and further it is also gentlemen one of the most important statement. It's not totally sure that's you all of you be a officiar's in Indian Army but it's sure you will be hold the authority you will be a powerfull person of the country so you will know the condition of India Army like some one became I.A.S., I.P.S. or any top class of beaurocartes some one became top business man some one become celebraty of the country that's time in the future please do not ignore the indian Army always remember that's you all of you a part of a Gorkha's rifles so in the future if any soldier hanging in any problem by economically or in any problem so you should be fully support to Indian Army with in both condition, in war or in peace because Indian Army full trusting on your self you are not a civilian you have wear a uniform you all of you a cadet for life time so he finished his speech and announced the name of medal winner so they consequently every cadet face to infront of colonel sir. They made first saluted him than he all ready stand within attention so after he decorated our uniform with medal.

So with in his last speech he was told that you all of you trained with Gorkha so we are providing you a medal to all of you this medal is a memories of life time that you are a part of this regiment so after medal distributing colonel sir made a plan for visit to us in Army officer's mess so he announce that today is our vacation and after lounch we will be visit the officer's mess. Than participate in evening game than celebrate the last successful evening of camp and tomorrow after breack fast you will be send in your college and lastly he was told that the twenty day's of training will be change your life may be some suffer in the today financial problem because you are a cadet and student but I am sure tomarrow you will be lead the country with in many different authority and department. You are a tomorrow future of Indian motherland. After speech colonel sir was valdication to every cadet and promised to in evening last night party. So after his gone our J.C.O NB/Sub Jagat Gurung Sir ordered us for visit the officer's mess that was a time 12 o' clock in noon. We all cadet moved for visiting the officer's mess on foot with consequently we moved for officer's mess with a ambition of our tommorrow dwel and place we were ambitious for visit the mess on foot we arrived at main gate of officer's mess where two Army men's stand for guarding the mess. They were healthy and more concious for their duty they guarding for their officer's mean their decision maker's they stoped us at men get by nimblty Captain Koushal Anand came from mess and he warmly welcomed us by their order we down our shoes at out side of mess door than we entered in officer's mess. That was assume the mess was fully five star hotel where every facilities was available firstly we entered in the mess, the out side to inner side wall of mess was fully decorated by gallent sceneries which was memoris of every Gorkha officer's J.C.O. and Jawan achievement in war as well as in peace where also hang the scneris of Ex Field Marshal General Manekshah who was also from Gorkha Rifles captain Koushal Anand sir, teaches us about the all scenerics history of Gorkha's and their achievements that also a really wonderful experience of our life where we realy closely understood the life style and their achievement about of Gorkha's in the officer's mess main gate was made by expensive white lead and in inner side thus was made by specially tiles and decorated by marvals that more attractive than a five star hotel and the life style of officer's of Indian Army was unparalleled than any civilian they are more veritious person than any civilian bureuerat and celebrities.

After watching the whole sceneris and learning about the earlier history of Gorkha Rifles that was a time to veldication from a officer's mess with a new commitment of that we will come back to return after commission in the Indian Army.

So after watching the officer's mess we were consequently stand in the line and did the 20 minutes of exercise actually some cadet made noise in officer's mess that was totally against to military law because politely they convence one time if you will improve to your misschief activities that's fine other wise you should Nimble ready for further punishment so some cadet made comic satire in the mess that's why every cadet faces the punishment, because according to military rule of our commred's did any mistake it's mean their all team or company will be for punishment so after punishment we were consequently stand in the line and moved for Gorkha building on foot we arrived at Gorkha building at 3 p.m O' clock than we were completed the lunch than we take rest to the 6 p.m. O' clock because our training was finished result was out and every laborious cadet got the medal that day's in early morning included me.

So we were much glad and proud to achievement's and our eyes drop's the tear's of new achievement because we all fully remembered that our senior did not wanted to send us in the camp. So we take bed rest till the 6 p.m. we wake up and assemble in Gorkha Varandah where reported CO sir and captain Koushal that night every one danced and singing the song that night every Jawan of 1/IV Gorkha Rifles J.C.O. and two officers captain Koushal Anand and colonel N.S. Pana and every cadet from various colleges of Chandigarh was fully enjoyed that night our meal prepared in fire wood that night Jawan was really enjoyed they drunk alcohal and our J.C.O. and officer's was also drunk than they danced and concentrate on chicken so of with in night party we were learn some more Gorkha word that *hokki hoi na hoi*. So really enjoyed that night and eat the chicken, the chicken was specially prepared for our last veledication and that was very tasty.

So after dinner C.O. sir and captain sir gone away from Gorkha building and after that's we did our dinner and moved for our quartor in the charlee where we were three Jagdev Nawab and Atul assambale and we conversation to Adam Lepcha sir to late night than we switched off at 11.30 p.m. that night we drooned in deep sleep because their were responsibility for another day's and in morning we wakeup at like earlier right time and followed the morning assambale in parade ground and running of five kilometer like other day's than morning pared with J.C.O. Jawan and officer's we all cadet became more active than previous time then we consequently moved for Gorkha mess where we did our morning breakfast. Than assemble in pared ground where captain Koushal sir was all ready attended in the pared ground who leads we all NCC cadet that day's captain sir was more delighted because who also became success in command us that was a time of 10 a.m. captain sir was in military uniform and decent looked he ordered us a comic punishment we all are bend and did puss up he was told that your exercise will be continue till the end of my cigarete fog and he began counting to not consequently.

We were tired but feel that we have a super energy our moral was so high because we made a history for our college. We are winner after punishment Koushal sir was distributed his contact Number to every single cadet for touch in the future than he veledication to us and gone away from Gorkha ground remain was NB/Sub Jagat Gurang and every N.C.O provided us green military colour of combat bus and we veledication to every Jawan and N.C.O. and J.C.O. Jagat Gurang they had moist eyes. But we committed to every one for always met with them time to time our presence in Gorkha s building was very pleasure experience for them because whole year they spended time away from their family so our presence unthrilled them like their children and brother. So we all cadet from D.A.V. assemble and we collect our luggage and sit in green military colour of combat bus with two Gorkha's Jawan our driver started bus and within some time we were a journey of new achievement's new responsibility and gain a new experience. That was totaly different than any other civilian life where strictness was comparatively to death life but the benefit of that strictness was more pleasure than a paradise. Where every thing and activities of combat men at the right time if some one acclimatrize to their self acording to Indian military rule no any other organisation better for them on earth and if some one could not acclimatrise to their self they faces many punishment you should be follow the rule and follow the procedure according to Indian Military so after that's we crossed main gate of western head command of Chandigarh we stand to our sit and saluted the western head command with nimblty that was a assume experience of our life and really we all remember till the end of our life, then our bus was running on the road crossed the panchkula and many sector of Chandigarh finally we entered in sector 10D to our college gate where all ready attended our senior.

Really they feel shy on the their previous attitude against on our self and they realy disturb and began to aware that no substitude of hard work where their is hard work determination wisdom their is way.

So we shake hand with them because they are our senior in our department it's mean our victory was not only for a single cadet it was for every one of my college and Batallion they really appreciate about us actually they were wards of Army officer's so they had a wrong thought that any other can not best performance but that day's they realise and made friendly behave to us than they retired from NCC and given charge on us they began to do the hard work for their commission in the Army because that time they are student and NCC cadet Mayank Badotra, Vijendar Singh Gill and Sivendar Pandey sir was more focused for commission, Pandey Sir and Badotra sir was always S.S.B out and Gill sir was could not cleared the entrance exam but they never gone back down continued their hard work for commission.

In our college our senior in NCC and other student had made their girl friend. But merely some one serious for marriage they are only enjoyed to her and wastage their energy and money with each other they always motivated me for made a girl friend but I was from rural area's and easily could understood about it's result I had friendly behave to every girl but not made any particular girl friend but I was seen our senior always misuse the relation to their girl friend, they are only playing with their relations, honour, dignity and respect to every girl they always cheated the girl and they represented to themselves to wrong identity like many cadet told the girl that they are Army officer's and they want to get marry (with them so girl was easily made their relation to them and whenever they loosed their relation to them and whenever they loosed their virginity and after uses they leave them then go for another girl and many one thing is common in girl was hang in their plan easily they could not understood one thing is common in today's girl is becoming greedy she could not understood the value of virginity, they wanted to secure prosperous life partner it's does not big matter who is old or young their are no value of education their are so value of only money and their it's mischief thought fully spail to their dignity chastity, virginity and self-respect in earlier time and now-a-day's it's totally against to Indian culture, custom and tradition. Every youth of the country can use of beautiful girl but merely some youth will be ready for marry the lost virgin girl. Virginity is a dignity of Indian soil in ancient time, foreign people of western country knowing India to it's own culture and culture is a influence of the girl of Indian their chasting and virginity if some on lost virginity before the marriage it means they are unresponsible for their husband, the western culture is fully spreading in India and its totally polluted to our culture. I am not against to right of Indian girl but I am conscious about the virginity, dignity and chastity of Indian girl.

I can not become Swami Vivekanand because who was salivate by birth but will try to become a saint like Maharshi Valmiki because who was dacoit but when he knows the value of truth he surrender to his every mischief and bad activities to god and devoted himself for truth, pure and light path by his hard devotion for god and he repents sincerely to god then god have mercy upon him and he is became a writer of Ramayan, a pure epic's of Hinduism.

So after the Army attachment camp I was became fame in batalion. For deserving cadet so I joined, O.T.A. attachement camp where I know that the girl friend making is also a quality of Army officer's so after returned from O.T.A. complete in February, I was in Shimla where I was proposed to Nicee Sharma for becoming my particular girl friend and she accepted my proposal and within two day's of compulsion finally I was invited her at my 21 birthday's in Shimla. She came at bus stand and made me a call I was received her then moved for movie watching that time the new released movie *billu barbar* she was very beautiful and healthy, she had parrot nose, we were in journey of mountain Queen City, Shimla, Himanchal Pradesh transport entered in theater. It was my first time with any girl. I was little bit hesitated but not nervous because I was fully trained in earlier O.T.A. by our officers, she sit very closely with me their were both chair was fully attache like other Cinema hall, the movie began and within movie time she pushed my hand by forcely I was excited after one hour's of movie she stuck my body to her left hand and pussed my hand to her right hand so I was became sexually excited so I began suck to her neck so I was became crazy and fully tied her hand to my body and I was began to sucking her neck with we totally droned in deep joy of young age. I began to puss her bubs and sucked her neck but I pointed out that some audience made eyes glance at our activities so she released me for some time but our mischief activities was not totally stopped but it was happening gradually.

So after finished the movie I was told her do not go away from the hall or theater after movie with in few time the whole theater was soly lock. I was utilize the solylock and made kisses to kisses on her neck and she was closely tied me with her hand I began to suck bur bubs, and pusses but gradually audiences came for another shoue so I stopped the mischievious activities and take a plan to rewatching the movie she was also agreed on my proposal. She sat on her chair and I collected the ticket from window.

Then we rewatched the movie of *billu barbar*. I restarted the mischief with her and she was glad to my mischievious activities she never ignored, or avoid she was fully supported my every activities.

After the movie when we came outside the theater, the shining day's was turned into dark evening we began to walk on Mall road. Actually that night was 14 Feb and my birthday's so we entered in National Coffee House on Mall Road. That's a famous for coffee in the Shimla, after two cups of coffee she decided to vilediction to me I was told her that night was my birthdays so I want to live with her. So she made a call to her parents and told that she will stay with her girl friend's so we began to walk to Mall Road I was stayed in Comfart Guest House and the manner of guest house became my friend because always in the Shimla travel. I made Comfart guest house to my dwell. So I made a call to him for night stay with a girl he agreed and on the way of Mall Road to our guest house were situated a good restaurant where we did our dinner than we moved for our comfart guest house before arrival to our dwell I was made a call to manager who told me for yes you can in our room I was with Nicee Sharma who was Punjabi Brahaman. She was very beautiful and fair girl that was my first night with any girl. I was sexually aggressive and she was also when we entered in the room close the door and switched off the our mobile and room light then she changed her clothes. She was in blue jeans and woolen and Shimla was more cool she became nude and I was also, physically she was very close to me I was very aggressive and that was very lusty night.

I was stuck with Nicee Sharma that was my first experience with any girl she was totally drowned in enjoy of my body she sucked my body. I was not obey her for suck my lips but she sucked my secret organ's.

I was drooned in deeply enjoyed really it was pleasure experience.

My body was very slim. She fully enjoyed with myself. I was sucked her every thing but not her secret organ's. As bab's she began to suck my penis I was out of my self feel like heaven, delighted myself.

Full night we were a wake, we really enjoyed sexually the lusty night. It was my first time but she was fully sexually satisfied with me that was a secrasy achievement's of my life which I won at the age of 21 six time my dispersal the sperm but I was not fell weakness that fully sexually satisfied the night was turn into dark shining a day's I was not slept and she was closely stucked with my body and did not wanted to release me, she told me that Atul you are really quite and I do not want to go away from your body.

I fully sacrificed for you. But please do not release me, otherwise I will not live she was told me that she really loved me. In morning 5 a.m. I was a sexually agressive and reused her sexually, she crying but loved me and she wanted then I told her the night turn into day's so go away because your parents were waiting for you. She did not wanted to release me but with thousand of commitment she was agreed for report at their home she goes away from the Comfart guest house and my virginity was no more. It was loosed at the age of 21. At that age Alexander became a king of Athense.

And in that age I was loosed my virginity, full night she was nude in the morning she weared her cloths and became very sainty, she became very close to me arrived at home she just made me a call hey dude, I am at my dwelling wake up and, fresh, then take a breackfast because today you are not a single you are engaged with me so it's my responsibility. I replied fine I will be also abule for you I do not worry. So after this experience, within few days I left Shimla. I left for Chandigarh when I was reported in my college my comrades had complaint to me because I was not celebrated my birthday's with them.

But to my close comrades Suryadeep and Yatin Saroha I was told that incident they became surprised.

But whenever I was remain in alone I thought that how she made physically relation with me because according to Indian culture custom and tradition the virginity is an ornament of every girl and one who be a Shylock it mean she turn into in new other identity. I am never against to woman's right, widow can marry, woman should represent every sector of country and society, they should be a well educated. They should be get employed, and be a self dependent she can join Indian defence forces as a combat commission officer but she do not need to loosed her virginity before the marriage and once she married she should be fully loyal for her husband, because now-a-day's criminal cases is increasing day by day in our society because in many cases woman having a physical relation to another person, that's actually many Indian enable to control to their self and spreading domestic violence to day by day because Indian mentality never offer to permission this type of hated relation and if some one became habitual to this type of relation they should do not go for marriage and otherwise if they want to marry with some one so they should be fully improve to his previous mischief and further it is also. This type of community people should be always ready for punishment by their life partner because whenever they knows, their previous relation, they feel guilty and the result of this mischief may be a harmful.

For their family so if some one making a girl friend and want to complete their sexual desire. They should be attention and if after uses if they want to leave her so they should be aware that his real life partner is also using by some one in some where.

So Nicee became very serious for me but I was fully focus on my studies she always made me many call but merely time I was free because, many times I was busy in Athelets and in my studies or with a company of my friends so daily I was made a call her in night she had many complain to me why you did not had sufficient time for me. I convinced her. But she was angry with me but after long conversation she became satisffied always she requested to me for Shimla visit but alway's I made any new excuse because after that I did not wanted to made physical relation, it was only a joy of few time and wastage of thrown.

Of time and money but it was complusion of young age with in study period in Chandigarh. I have seen with very clearly merely a girl was virgins and chasty in urban area's because my every command's had a girl friend's some one have the four or five girl friends without any hesitation but I could not acclimatise to myself in this type of culture, I mean how you can dominate a girl who was already enjoyed an old relation it mean she was slave of a men and who was thrown her and you catched but my thought was totally different that I will make a life partner who was never enjoyed the sexual life with some one because in those condition.

I will be a king of her life because in her vision she have only man and that is me.

It will be a pleasure experience So I saw in aristocratic society virginity was merely but in cultured aristocratic family present it so it's totally depend on their culture.

So gradually my every comrade know about my relation to Nicee because in the Ist week of March in 2009 she made a travel of Chandigarh. I was met her with my charm friend Yatin Saroha. She was told me that all but I was convince her for it. She told me she want to leave within living relationship. I was strickly worn that it may be not possible so I was veldication to her from Chandigarh and she gone away for Shimla but Yatin Saroha save her number she alway's made me a call but I could not pick up her call. So my friend's asked her to friendship but she was strickly worn her that she only love's to Atul Kumar Pandey my many friend's made her call but she never accepted their proposal but Yatin Saroha closely attached with her.

Because I was gone away from her life. I was not attended her call when I was not attended her call she made a call to Yatin Saroha regard's asked about myself gradually they mentain relation.

Their relation increasing, but I made a call and strickly adviced her. I was told and convince her what happen with us forget these all but please do not create any other relation in your life always wait for your marriage because your husband will be your real life partner so do not loose your dignity with any another and I will be alway's for you till the end of my life. She was of my life. She was cried and told me she will never forget me I told her. Absolutely I will also.

But after one years Yatin told me she became very serious about myself and they create physical relation with each other. I was very guilty and angry about her because I live remain single without her but she made a new relation with some one and did the one year ago she was told me that she loved me. Where is gone her spirifual love.

So due to the effect of time my senior becoming Army officer like Vijendar Singh Gill Sir, recomanded for O.T.A.

Chennai and Komal Sir who earlier joined the camp Gorkha with and who became best shooter within six include I and every one was also becoming serious for their goal.

So my college day's was also over and finally to the activities of urban girl I was decided to make a life partner in rural area's because in the hop of where the girl preserve their shy chastity and virginity and girl lived under cover so I was moved for Dehradun.

So after my college day's in Chandigarh I was moved to Dehradun prepare for commission in the Armed force's fully committed sacrifice for. Studies by train Gorakhpur junction to I arrived Dehradun, where situated officer's acadmy was more fame coaching for N.D.A. and C.D.S. Actually I had NCC C certificate so I did not need to take the written test, I can join Direct SSB but this opportunity only providing for O.T.A. not for I.M.A. so for better opportunity I made journey for officer's academy.

Where I was very serious about studies I stayed in Garhi cant the classes began at 10 a.m. ends at 2 p.m. and the distance of any dhaba was more than 2 kilometer and in morning time they could not prepare breakfast. So I joined the class every day without breakfast and we were came back to our P.G. (Personal guest at 3 p.m. that time lunch was not possible any where in Garhi cant, because they finished till the 4. o clock and I was join a English classes 4 p.m.-6 p.m. I was came back to return P.G. at 3.30 p.m. and English classes going till 4 p.m. so with in half an hour's lunch was not possible so that time only dinner was possible. But their were many thing good for learning. Like Pritam Sir was fully devoted for his teaching duty and for English coaching Geeta Mam both are good teacher's.

In the Geeta Mam classes many girl came for English coaching but in these all girls, a girl came whose name was Neha. She was most beautiful than others and I noticed her. She made me eye contact but I did not care because I did not wanted to made any girl friend because I was fully aware to it's result. And I wanted to became a Army officer then I will go for marry in rural areas because I thought that the girl of rural areas is more cultured, traditional and main thing is that they preserved their virginity till the marriage.

I thought if she will come from lower family even poor family. Even if she will not very beautiful I will never complain to her.

Because money and physical charm will destroy to the effect of the time.

But spiritual beauty makes woman more beautiful for ever. So I concentrated on my studies where whole day's I was busy in Pritam sir. officer's academy then Geeta Mam in night till the 1 p.m. till 2 p.m. I had very limited time for bed Rest with one month I did very hard work the duration of course in officer's academy was three month. So in the month of May the result came of C.D.S. exam, my many comrades was seen there exam result and further it is also I was also did the entrance exam before joining the course at officer's academy but my paper was not so good. That's why I did not wanted to cheek it. But one senior was asked me my roll no. I was told so that was surprised I cleared the C.D.S. entrance exam. and my S.S.B. was began soon in the month of June 2012, at 19 Board Allahabad.

That was the time and places was decided.

So it was last week of May and the S.S.B. was decided in second week of June. So my more time spend in Dehradun was not better for my S.S.B. preparation. So I pluck the course in Dehradun and moved for Chandigarh with Himachal Pradesh Travel.

In Chandigarh my charm friend Suryadeep was stayed regarding Law entrance exam preparation so I was reported in Chandigarh where we three friends Suryadeep, Chayan Chahal, and Atul was decided to visit the whole Northwestern Himachal Pradesh. So we started our journey from Chandigarh to Dharamshala we visited many places, Buddha temple where Dalai Lama staged. Neelkanth peak where Maeklodgang where the climate was cool in the month of June when other plain burning than Palampur, Dalhoujee that was super journey, after journey. I came back to my home town Kushingar because my SSB was decided at Allahabad and distance between Kushinagar to Allahabad is more closer than Chandigarh.

18 June was the date of my SSB I made journey by train in the II A.C. from Gorakhpur to Allahabad.

At 17, I was reported at Allahabad stayed in Hotel. At 18 I was entered in S.S.B. Board it's a dream's when I was in very earlier age for becoming a combat officer's that was becoming true. By hard work and determination first day's in Board they were treated us by gentle manner's one night was stayed in S.S.B. board where fooding lodging every thing was free of cost for cadet, next day's in the morning was our screening exam. Actually the procedure of SSB is five day's and if some crack the five day's they will selected for officer's in the Indian Army.

In next days comprises 20 of batch I mean 20 cadet discuss about one Matter and only two are screen in my group I was screen out.

They send me at first day's I came back at my dwelling at Kushinagar. I was upset because in the first attempt. I could not reconend. In the Indian Army I was preparing for next time. So that time I was upset and really I wanted to made any girl friend who are virgin, cultured because I wanted to turn my relation to marriage.

So a beautiful girl was staged in my neighbour's town, the distance between my town to her town was 35 kilometer's. I was in Hata Kushinagar, and she was stayed in Gorkhapur. My family knows her, always told that she is very cultured and traditional type of girl.

She did her M.A. in Hindi. Many times I made a comment's about her but my family, like sister, and mother told me she never gone away from the home. Actually she lived with her real elder uncle, aunty cousin, she was basically from rural areas, but stayed in Gorakhpur regarding study's purpose.

Once upon a time I crossed her gully and seen her, she was very beautiful, parrot nosed, and they are still typical brahmin family.

Actually my family known her family, her elder uncle was school teacher in government school in Gorakhpur. And her cousin was a student of B.Sc. (medical)

So they had joint family remaining member of family was stayed in her remote village, her name was Pinkee and the name of her uncle was Ramesh and her cousins name was Vinay. My family alway's talking about their family because master ji was seven brothers it's a nuclear family. But they never quarrel to each other.

They had very acrimonious relation in their family, my family was told me about Pinkee She had five sisters, no real brother's, her mummy and her other sisters stayed in her remote village.

Once upon a time I asked to my family about Pinkee to know about any boy friend but my sister replied. She is very decent and no one could blame about her character. She is pure salivate, virgin. She preserved her chastity like her ornament you came from urban areas thats why you have this type of rediculus thought my sister was told me that she is brahman and without gods reptend she never did her breakfast. She is pure typical and more traditional. My sister continued her speech about her, no doubt about her chestity and virginity. My whole family very appreciate about her work and her every activities. So my heart was extremely delighted and I wanted to contact with her. So many time I was decided to visit the master ji house but in earlier time never I did. So I thought to visit master ji's home. They will see me a dubious eyes and they will keep their eyes on myself. Because they are more decent and traditional brahamin family and I was in the compulsion of young age, the people have many complain about young age. So in many questions came in my mind and I was canall the plan but I was fully effort for urgest the number of Pinkee. Fortunately my niece passed High School from my home town for his further studies their were no English medium Intermediate school so my sister and my family decided to send him in Gorakhpur for his further studies so my nefew participated in many entrance exam but he was cleared only a English medium school that school was situated in little bit outside of Gorakhpur so their were no residence facilities for him so it's a problem I also searches many places for his dwelling but no one was superior so after facing the many problem their were no any places for his resident. Once upon a time my family known the school was more close to master ji's home. So they are asked him to stay my nephew with them and master ji was agreed he was accepted. So my nephew send at master ji's home. It's a golden opportunity for me to talk to Pinkee.

So after his arrival at the home of master ji. Once alway's I made a call to my nephew once I call him but nephew forgeted his mobile at the home. So Pinkee picked the call I was told can I talk to Suraj she was told me. Actually I am Pinkee and Suraj leave his mobile it dwelling. It's a better chance to talk to her. I was told her, hello, Pinkee she use totally pure Hindi word, her language so weathy and her voice was so nice it's very sweet voice she told me.

Actually whenever he will arrive at home then will inform him about your call, but I was continued talk to her. I said do not worry Pinkee if he is not here so you can talk to me. She was not replied but by politely asked what are you doing she was told me nothing, I said why she was replied that my elder uncle is in his school and Suraj is also in the school and her cousin was away from the home I asked her how you handle these all responsibilities like making food for them and doing student she replied it's not big deal. It's my job. So I wanted to continued that conversation I asked what is you doing she was replied actualy this year I am totally free because I did my master's in Hindi but could not secure good mark's for. Further PhD. programme so she did not wanted to continued long conversation then told me actually I had some domestic work. If you do not mind I can cut the call I replied sure but I will like to talk to you. So how I can contact you. She told me actually it's totally wrong if you want to talk to me so you can call me at Suraj's number. But I do not like it. So I passed smile then requested her regard's talk to me in the future so she told me ok you can call me only at Saturday's night then she cut the phone.

I was flying in the sky became very glad and really it's a achivement's that a traditional cultured girl was talking to me that was Monday's and I waited for Saturday night. So in the waiting for his call the day's was very restic and night was so long. I feel a day turn into night like a year turn into another year. But my heart was so delighted that when I remembered her last sentence that you can call me only at Saturday night. But I was satisfied because I wanted to made her as a life partner and she was a maiden mean pure chest and virgin girl. And their are no doult about her character that time. I feel alone because I was S.S.B. out from Indian Army. So I had a new meaning for my happness that's reason and I wanted to full effort for my upcoming S.S.B. but which decided after six month so I had sufficient time for rest and I was tired because long time I spended in my studies.

So I made a journey for watching the movies and in travel so and waiting in the call of Pinkee her impact was on myself was assume I always smiled without any reason and waiting for Saturday night mainly she was fully forefiet me. A long waiting for Saturday night finally came that night. It's a 7 p.m. evening time. I made a call to my nephew Suraj. He picked my call. I asked about him-self and stand twenty question about his studies and residence in master ji's home. He was replied that every thing is fine and about his meal and residence was also comfort he told me that his meal was prepared Pinkee aunti. She was very careful about him. So I told him that forward the mobile to Pinkee and I wanted to talk to her so he forwarded her. She told me in pure Hindi and in traditional with very respectful word hello ji, I asked how are you she was told fine, and what about you. I replied I was good, but now I am not good she told why, I replied that I have a very extreme attachement with you and always I missing you and you were told me for waiting the Saturday night. Do you know's how I crossed the every rustic day's and long night than come this golden evening. I was told her actually I want to friendship with you. Only friendship because I have a attachment to you. She was replayed that this attachment is very dangerous do not goes in deep control to yourself and take care about you and so I asked how are you. She was told me well I asked why you given me a time for long Saturday night and in evening she was told me nothing actually every day's I had overburden of tomorrow but at Sunday I am still staying free. So I can given you time in Saturday night because for next day's I have no extra burden. Because next days everyone will stay at home so I could make the meal late to another day's so asked how you acclimatised to yourself in the room. You do not have a desire to watch the movie or travel anywhere so she told me I am a girl and the chastity is my dignity so I replied what is the relation between watching the movie and decline the chastity, she replied it's your thought because long time you spending in urban area's but the thought my family and my surrounding people is very traditional that without marriage or without their parents we can not gone away from the home understand, I am a girl, I am not a boy.

Grown in cultured traditional rural brahamin family. So there are so many restrictions and responsibilities to us. I talk to you it's total against to our law, because as a girl of traditional family I have no recognisation for talk to any one. Who is away from our family. But I replied that your family is known my family so how you can say's that's I am away from your family. She replied that's why I talked to you. Otherwise I never prefered that our conversation I passed smile with that she influence of very traditional and cultured girl and I am very lucky to contact with her. I asked so what are you doing she told me that I have to go to prepare the dinner so if you do not mind can I cut the phone. I told her can you give me your personal contact number.

She replyed please give me some time for thought about it, I was told her when we will began talk to each other easily we can understand about each other. I smiled and told offer me your contact will be esiest for me if Suraj switch of his mobile. If any time the mobile of my nephew will be switched off so she was smiled and told me that you can call at my elder uncle's number or my cousin's number. I was laughed she was also involve in the company of my laughter then she was silence I asked, it's my second day's and what type of wrong word used for you she replyed nothing I asked so why you have hastiation to provide me your presonal contact number she was smile nothing because every time my elder uncle, anuty and my cousin is available here. I replied after passing the number whenever you will be free then make me a miss call then I will call you. She was replied ok but given me some time for thought please, I replied do you known how I can wait the rustic day's and long night will be come back to return Saturday's night she replied give me one opportunity gradually the duration of our conversation was converted into hour's she replied it's late night I have need cute the phone please call back me at Saturday's night I was frustate but had no another subtitute she veldication to me ok good night I was also replied then she cut the phone. After her veldication I was missing her. Every thing her sweet voice, her face because once I crossed the her gully and seen her. Before our conversation.

She was very quite and her behave was internally praise my heart what I wanted she was better than my thought I was drowned in her dream and tried to waiting for next

Saturday but it was very sustic for me I thought if I had super-natural power I changed week into within a second but it was not possible it was fact that waiting for next Saturday's night because I had no another option. So I involved myself in any work because whenever I busy in some work I was not forget her but my concentration was just lost on Pinkee and it was focused on the work but not fully it was happened.

First time I was hanged in the compulsion of a pure virgin, chasting girl who was a influence of rosey check moral lips and star like eyes these all make her more beautifull. I wanted to fully devotion for her because I did not wanted to loosed her in any condition because I cam from a Arban area's I did my college in a aurostaratic society where merely a girl preserve her virginity till the marriage.

But she was merely a girl who are more traditional fully aware about the culture of motherland the rule and regulation of indian motherland she well know's she born in a country where acording to our epic's without marriege loosed virginity or, sexual relation sign's it's not a our backwordness it's our advancement because acording to science cardeta species is a well devolped creature on the earth and Home sapiene is a more powerful or, wiser than other creature they can understand about the value of relations they can different in their relation. They can mentain the understanding in their family because they are gniees that's why our epics is pure it's fully strict us that do not order us for be a animal should be understand to the right and wrong way and I was glad because I choosed a life partner who was virgin according to our epics and science. So I was watching for a Saturday night when she will be available for talk to me I did not known why but alway's I wanted to listen the voice of Pinkee.

There were some girl made me a call but after attachment with her, I ignored every call of in many beautiful girl because I wanted to become a more I to Pinkee, loyal wanted to vistied intire world but not only with Pinkee many dream's and ambition was playing in my brain. I was waiting for Saturday night but this wait is delighted my heart. In the ambitional of a life partner I became more deserving than previous time. I concentrated for my work because I had no more desire to any another girl of a whole world. But because what I wanted got it the time is infinite if you enjoying it's just finish a night like with in a minutes. But it will be more long when you waiting for something.

And it will be more long when you will be wiating for special some one so that time I was waiting for a special someone so the night was so long for me and day's was more rustic, Saturday night is up coming but I feel a day converted in to a year's because.

My desire to Pinkee is increasing to day by day. My face was more shining and the people told me that's I am handsome but I did not wanted to waste my physical charm for every one I wanted to utilize it with a special some one. I feel that I will be alway's available for special some one.

Finally to the effect of time and long waiting procedure, Saturday night came when a virgin, chasting and beautiful girl was available talk to me. I was called to my nephew in 7 p.m. evening and asked him to his condition and his every activities in his new deweling than his fooding he was told me that pinkee auntee is very caring about me and every thing is very comfortable. So I asked do you have any problem can you consult to pinkee I was told him that call forward to the Pinkee he was transfered mobile to Pinkee. She speak Hello. I was told that good evening mam. She was told me that good evening sir, suddenly I became very emotional and told my every condition to her. I told her feel very extremely attachment to you. and the waiting of these long evil's day's is very rustic for me and I am anable to control myself to waiting these long day's give me your personal contact number she was passes smiled and told that you easily you can know about myself from Suraj or any other relative so why you want to take my personal contact number you knows I stayed within the family where I am alway's busy and the rules and regulations of my family is more strict if someone knows. I am only talk to you it will be very harmful for us.

I convince her that I am not a ridiculous a I am a B.Sc student and NCC C Certificate holders if some one make critissm against us a I will convence them because I am not like careles so if the member's of yours family if aware about these all incident they do not make any comments against as you do not think like that but she was very decent and cultured the passing her presonal contact number was like a crime for her. She did not wanted she told me. She respect me but I am, in the compulsion of my family I will knows you are also a very cultured but you should understand about my compulsion.

She continued her speech she told me that your voice is also very sweet and praise my heart I want to contineue to conversation with you but I am hanging the compulsion of my traditional and cultured family she become very emotional and told her personal contact number and advised me that whenever I will be give you a miss call. Then make a call otherwise do not make any call to me. I was very glad and like it was my victory on the star's and moon so it was praise my heart than she was told me for do not mind. and I have to go for cut the fone and I told her that when I will make a call for you she was told me that after 11 p.m. I will be fully free then will give miss call then you will call back me. So it was 7.30 p.m. in evening and I was waiting for night 11.30 p.m. for her conversation. I completed my general studies then dinner, but my heart beat was more sounding because it was first chance for me when I will talk to her in the long conversation.

After more waiting it was 11.30 p.m. I was call her she pick my call and told that every one completed their dinner but even I have to go for it. So do not mind call back me within half an hours so I become angry. But further it is also I tryid to understand her situation that she had many responsibility. Like every domestic work to making the food and care of every one these all responsibility was on her shoulder that's why I was waiting for her so gradually the time was spended and watch was going on 12 o' clock then I made a call her. She was pick up my call and told that actually she was did tooth brush then told me for talk to me within fifteen minutes. So again was prepared to myself for waiting and it was excess waiting for some one and every men of the world in this condition generally become angry on but I was convince to myself that it is happening because she is holding many responsibilitis she is very responsible for her family. Then after waiting of half an hour's I made a call her she was picked my call and told that I am really apologise for these long waiting actually tomorrow is not overburden because upcoming Sunday. I am habitual of everyday for finished the work at the right time because in the morning breakfast is very necessary on the right time that's why I completed it. So please do not mind it I convince myself that she is very chasting and cultured girl and she did her every work at the right time I began to talk to her, I asked her Pinkee daily how you get a time in the mid night how you acclimatise to yourself because where no one for your help in the cooking or any domestic work but further it is also your effort for your family. It is a great sacrifice and I am sure merely a handful girl will ready to live a life like it. She was again told me cheerfully that do not be emotional it's my work and I am habitual for it since last five years let's began talk to each other she asked me how are you I passed smile very good because to night to you offered me your contact Number that's why. She was asked me why you wanted talk to me. I told her every one have a desire for a life partner who is more loyal, more honest and more chasting for them. I was also desired for it. Long time I spended in urban area's where merely a girl who follow the rule of Indian motherland that's a rule of cultured traditional and virgin girl the majority of people demanding only not a pure traditional cultured and virgin girl but my thought is totally different the hafety amount of dovery will be decline to the effect of time. But spiritual beauty is a influence of cultured traditional chasting and virgin girl's will be forever for your reason of your wealthy, healthy and happy family.

So people can make the lots of many by hard work, determination, and by wisdom but man can not create a traditional and cultured girl it will be created only by a healthy and culture society.

I wanted talk to you because you are a beautiful and intillegent it's your extra quality which is gifted by god that's why I wanted to talk to you first I want to friendship with you. You are ready or not she was silence but told yes so commited for our good friendship so she was asked which quality of a girl you more like. I told her a group of a major people of Indian society having a desire for traditional wiser chasting virgin loyal honest these all thing's are very important for any Indian girl and every scholar having a desire for their life partner to these all Quality who could mentain she was asked me about her physical charm I told her every beautiful physical charm will be decline to the effect of time but sense of responsibility, loyalty, honesty, virginity, chastity make a woman more beautiful, physical charm can attract of the people only for limited time but when the passing of time people search in the woman her loyalty, honesty, sense of responsibility, sense of honour's that's why Indian woman should be liberate but they do not need to decline their her virginity and chastity and and give a statement that, I am more advance, it's not a symbol of advancement if before marriage, if some one loosed their virginity without any accident by her desire so. She will be knowing by other name in our society, So I appeal to every woman and men to Indian soil that's they should be preserved their virginity till the marriage because it will be mentain your dignity, chastity and self-respect in the society.

So every girl should understand it but unfortunately many girl decline her chastity in the compulsion of young age because western culture totally spreading their culture in Indian society so our culture is poluting day by day and it's a responsibility of Indian youth that's they need understand it. preserve your virginity and preserve your culture. She was listening with concentration.

She appreciated about myself and told that she was very lucky having I friend like me because your thought is totally Indian thought I told her that always I listen about you appreciated about yourself than I wanted to contact you but due to the effect of time, I could not contact you but it's my fortunate that attache with you so with in our conversation the time was crossing the 3.30 a.m. so I told her for veldication and committed for call in the early morning. So I told that night.

So in the early morning I wake up at 10 a.m. so after bathroom brush I made a call and she picked my call. After a respect to good morning we began our conversasion to each other I had many friends and many people who trusted on me.

Whenever they were hanged in any problem they requested me for their solution infact in any problem they requested me for exact judgement but that time I was totally busy to with Pinkee she became my goal extra time and I had no my every regard's involve in the any matter. So each and every day's I made a call to Pinkee in the night 11.30 p.m to morning 4 a.m. but in my previous life I never became addicted to these type of activities but really became habitual talk to her. Without listen her voice nothing was good for me but after our converstion my heart was become deighted with her. Voice was very peaceful that touched my internal heart and unthrealed me a new energy.

Their are merely people turn their dream's into reality and I was one in these all merely people because I wanted a traditional life partner and finally I got Pinkee as a option for my future so our conversation was on the boom once a night I called her and told that. Pinkee actually without talk to you every thing is fade for me and I do not knows why but I have realy a very close effection to you. I feel I fell in the true love with you she was very silence and I was very emotional but she told me realy you are a nice guy's for me but our love relation is not. Good I asked her really you feel me that you love me or not she told me really I love you to more so I was given her uncounting kiss on the cell and she was also started. I said without you I can not live I feel you are my body organ's she replied that you are also a part of my life. She told me that I am very fortunate you were met me without lots of effort. I wish to thank god and my parents that you are as a my lover. I kissed her many time on the cell phone and she was also started so our kissing was became a compulsory part of our conversation.

When she talked to me passed the uncounting kiss and whenever I feel that the any kiss was not strong I was ordered her that repeat again every day we began talk to each to 9 a.m. to 11 p.m. than we take rest of half an hour's for our breakfast then we started till the 2 p.m. then we take a rest lucnch and the rest of half an hour's than we started to 2.30 p.m. to 6 p.m. then we take a rest for evening tea to one hour's then we started to 7 p.m. to 10 p.m. in the night then we take a rest for one hour's for our dinner, then we started 11 p.m. to 4 a.m. in the morning it's a indeed not a fake total we made near about minimum fifteen hours it was became my daily routine she was also made her. Routine it's a girl who never talk to any one and due to the effect of time fifteen hour's devotion for her love mind and heart and she was also fully fell in the love to the impact of her long conversation gradually her cousin was began to understand about her activities and she became fearless so her cousin protested her activities but she was straight forward replied him actually her cousin was additcted in eigarette fog and tobacco chewing but no one understood about his activities so whenever he was told that he will inform to every family member about her activities she replied that she also tell to all of them about his eigarette fog and tobacco chewing her cousin was very decent type of boy and alway's concentrate on his studies made a journey away from the home and join the coaching class that's why he did not had lot's of time for protest her, so she made her time utilising in her love ocean, she was fully drowned in the love with Atul Kumar Pandey. She never wanted to lived away from my conversation really we were very closely attach to each others my happiness was became her a reason of her happiness I did my B.Sc. in medical I wanted to became a doctor that's why I know every thing about our health, that long talking and long time to conversation in mid night became a reason for our neurological, psycological, chronic, and liver disease.

I known and suggested to every one do not awake in the late night because it will be very harmful for human being's but I was awaked at whole night. I was in the compulsion of young age and these age is also a very harmful than any other disease of the world and the list of W.H.O. and M.C.I. it's more dangerous disease and merely a real men can stop to their self to these strong disease. I was suggested to every one that do not awake and in the mid night but I was comit that mistake everyday's and everynight I did my B.Sc. in (medical) and I was NCC Certificate holder's from 2 Chandigarh batalion so should be more conscious about my health but my love with Pinkee forgeted every expensive degree and certificate which was I got from reputed instiution of India.

The disease of a young age is a step forward than any disease of world and which is listed in W.H.O. and M.C.I. and I became acute patient of young age who was totally drowned the ocean of love and my every relatives sat on surrounding the ocean and seen my love stories with Pinkee but we were very fearless and drowned with each other in the ocean of love.

Gradually we started share to our every problem, once I said her every problem once I said her Pinkee I love you, she replied I love you too dear, I said I want to suck your lips she replied. I was also suck your upper and lower both lips. I asked I want to sleep with you she replied that I am only for you forever so do not be hestitate I will always available for you. So I asked, we were talk to each other since with in one month but we never met face to face with each other so I want to meeting with you, she was replied that yes. I will meet you. I asked how where you can come. She replied that at 31 October no one will be stay at dwelling so you can come at my dwelling at 31 October 2012. I replied it will be major risk for us because entry in your home is not possible because after my arrival if some one suddenly come in your dwelling so in that condition what will happen.

She was replied do not worry actully your family know our family. So you are come in directly in my relation so no one will be asked this type of question. But I had a dignity and my self respect. So did not wanted to made a journey of her home. But she was forcely replied you can come here, because I am here stay since last five year, so easly can understand the it's real situation, so do not be tearing fearing hazitation with proudly you can come at my dwelling and I will be wait for you. I was upset but their are a compulsion of my self-respect family respect, and my dignity because their are no any question mark in my family about these type of activities because whenever I was in Chandigarh no fault I created a self-respect in Chandigarh so Chandigarh was my second home town that's why I was never commit any mistake. In Chandigarh it's my real home town where not everyone known me like Chandigarh where every student know that I am Atul Kumar Pandey. But their are a mystress of my family respect that's why I was hesetate. In previous time in Shimla no one know me that's why I was made a girl friend, and had a painful experience but wanted to turn this beautiful relation into marriage but without permission of her guardian how I could enterer in her twice and suppose some one come at that time than what I will do, I was not fearing to about my self the reason of my fears was my self respect because acording to Indian culture if some on loosed their self respect than who is equally of a dead body. But she was forcely convince me that no one could come at that time because I well known about them when they came when they can not come. So do not be a fear person come so I was decided for visit the her home and 31 October 2012 I was made plan to visit her home according to my decision I made a juurny of her home in Gorakhpur finally arrived at her gully and made a call her. She was convince me regard's direct arrival at home I was told that I am unable to come alone come and receive me so she was come infront of the gully was seen her. She had long height, parrot nose and fair colour she stand infornt of the gully. She was seen me but could not identify me because she never directly seen me. I made a call she told me I am infront of the gully besides the Diljeet Pan Bhandar, where are you I was told her. I am a step away from the Diljeet Pan Bhandar, I told her that I am in black colour shirt and blue jeans long heght 5.10 feet and was stand besides her she made eye glance in my eyes and I remembered that her eye never mispointed to in my eyes her eyes was very freety and I feel thousand of youngster could fall in her eye at the last to first time she never fall but I have fully remembered that finally I was fully fall in her eye her eyes was make killing's so every youth of the world and I was drowned in the ocean of her eyes. And I did not wanted to come back from her killing's eyes I had many girl friends only as a friend but never seen this type of killing eyes.

She awake up me for come in your consiousness me I tried to return in my consciousness and but not in fully consciousness she shows me the way of her home and told me to come home. I was replied if your elder aunty come so she replied do not worry I have everything cleared he is away from the home and minimum he will return with in one hours with fearly my internal soul never allowed me for entered in the room but my age forced me for just entered in her home. I became shylock and fearless, directly walking for her home she lead me and I was followed her subsequently she was two step forward than me and I was directly followed her so without any hazitation she was entered in the room and I was followed her I was also entered in her home I there were only two bedroom, kitchen and one bathroom, the areas of room was so broad, but further it is also I was hazitated that and asked to Pinkee with in only two bed room how you could acclimatize to your self because their are three men, your elder uncle, your cousin Suroj and two women you and your auntee where who sleep so she was guided me that my elder uncle and my cousin sleep in one Bedroom, and in one room their are two bed and surely I had seen their were two bed in Pinkee's room, she told that I sleep in bed and at another bed sleep Suraj. So I was replied that master ji, Mr. Ramesh her elder uncle is teaching in government school and he is earning hafty amount per month other than you have large scale of agriculture field where you geting large amount of grain's every year. They should mentain it's all by these type of common problem of bedroom and further it is also it the really they do not have sufficient money so they should take bank loan for these reconstruction of building but the two bed room is not sufficient for your long nuclear family. She passed smile and replied that they are earning money it's fact but they are slow in the spending, they having only desire to collect the money and deposititin bank. I was also passed a smile, and told that they should be remember, they can not die with money they leave their all properties on the earth, she passed smile and we finished our conversation about two room of bed room she provided me sweet and a glass of water I cut half peace of sweet and half eaten her. Then I ship a glass of water. So suddenly she moved to kitchen for making the tea I was complain to her that do not make tea but she was not agreed of my proposal for preparing the tea, swear me for seep the tea and began to preparation tea in kitchen she was standing in kitchen I feel boring lonely in the room that's why I was also moved in kitchin I saw her physical structure was very attractive I touches her skin in the kitchen that was very soft then I forward my step to close her but she was agreed to my closeness I once again forward my step now I was very close to Pinkee than I was closely a stuck to the Pinkee and seen her face that was ver shining and fair her nail coloured in brown colour that made her more attractive. I closely stuck with her then I saw her face that was very fair her chuck was rosey and lips was very soft so I could not control to my self I began to sucked her lips within very dirty style I entered her lips in my mouth and began to sucked. She closely stuck with me and she also wanted I sucked her neck and pushed bubs she was aggressive and close stuck with me beginning the sucking of her lips was continued with suddenly that was became very lusty but we did not fulfil our sexual desire the vapour of tea was flow on the cylinder so we tried to return in consciousness I released her with her virginity you can not say's that she was no more chasting but she was virgin because I could not tried to spoil it because I did not wanted to loose that night she was fully trusted me and it was my responsibility to mentain her dignity so I released her and I sip a cup of tea and she was also sip then after finishing the tea. I began to suck her lips then return in consciousness and wanted to veldieation to her because the time of arrival of her uncle was so close, so after sip the cup of a tea a vildication to her she was agreed and told me that the arrival of her elder uncle time is so close than I veldication to her.

Before leaving to her I again stuck with her and tried to love with her began to suck her lips and her neck she was asked me when you will come back to return I replied that it will be dangerous for us so you will come in the complex then we will watching the movie with each other I was convinced her when you will go away from your home she was replied at every Saturday, after in evening so, I convince for next Saturday come before the right time of temple than we will watching the movie she began to suck my lips with in very dirty style than we stopped and veldication to each other and after velidication. I was come from her home than I was flying in the sky because I was closely attache to a virgin girl. I spoil chastity of a chasting virgin, traditional and culture girl I was very glad and really I wanted turn my relation into marriage. It was internally praise my heart.

I was very delighted because what I wanted I did it's victory on the star's and moon.

I feel I am a king of her body and her soul because she was closely love me and soul, because she was closely love me, trast me. She shear me her everything. She became a part of my life this achievement brought me a love energy. Before the relation to Pinkee I never to fell down in the love but really I was not only in the love I was drowned in the ocean of her love her delighting is my delighting. Her sadness was my sadness. Totally she became a internal part of my body and soul. She also captured my psycological and physical properties.

So after meeting with her? I celebrated the bithday's party of my nephew day after tomorrow I return at my home after that's meeting we became more lusty than earlier time we when from began our conversation it was happen with strong kissing. I asked her every lusty particles of her body and with cheerfully she replied. We wanted to live with each other. Because we had more desire for our physical satisfaction.

But really I did not wanted to loosed her virginity before the marriage, but further it is also I wanted to always watches her with my nude eyes without her presence every thing was fade forme meet so gradually our desire to meet with each other increasingly to day by day but with thousand of time I convince to myself waiting for her but the result was nothing I told everything. It was a compulsion of young age no one could control so as a human beings how it may be possible for me. So our conversation continued daily at the same time in each and every condition. So gradually I became very habitual to her then if she cut the phone between in our conversation I was became aggressive, and began abused to her but silently she was listen and did not replied any time but she had many responsibilities that time of every members of her family but with loyalty she always attend the call every time, and whole night she was busy on the call without any hesitation between our conversation period many problems was created that time but she always faces with gallantly, because gradually every members of her family was well known about she was fell in the love with me but and they made many strickness against her, but she was dare and told to her mother about me and her love she told to her mother that she was fell in the love and she would be going to marry me. Her mother supported her, gradually our desire to meet with each other on boom. So I was orderd her, meet tomorrow so she cheated them behind temple or other work arrived at temple where we were decided and many times we watched the movies.

In the watching of movie. The shining day's was turned into dark evening and that time she became a very frighten but facess that condition, and reported her dewelling at late evening where her real elder uncle asked many questions but she replied him alway's lie, and saved her every one knows about her activities but she never. So she always behave to them with gentle idea's and never made scene like she face to face meet with me, that's why they treating her. Normaly because they known, she is liable for punishment, because she was fell in the love with me but it's their unfortunate that they did not had any evidence against her and another side our romance was on the four top star. So after first meeting with her our sexual desire was on the boom so always I forced her. For our again meeting. But she always told that she did not had sufficient time because once earlier she meet me. Then they had doubt she did not had any other excuse once she told me at Sunday's. Her elder uncle will be gone away. From the home then I could meet with her.

So I made a plan for our Sunday meeting that time, the month of November but the sun shining and atmosphere was so hot, every where rustic climate in whole north India's and Gorakhpur is not exupteation but I was in a jouney of meeting with my beloved and in the ambition of meeting with her was on the boom and that time the rustic climate of whole north India and basicaly Gorakhpur was like a very pleasent climate for me humidity was on the boom due to the effect of subtropical climate of Gorakhpur in the effect of sun shining day's and burning ray's of sun was directly burn the skin of the people and a very minor group of people could seen on the road because the days was more burning more hot and more rustic but I was in the a joury of a meeting with my beloved I was fearless to the rustic climate of north India and made a joke on burning shining day's of sun because their every boundation was enabule to stopped me and I was moved for meeting with her. Lastly I was arrived at Gorakhpur and after arrival I made a call for her and I told her came and receive me because I did not known the mentality of her neighbour's so she came near about hundred meter's away from the home and received me, then she was two steps forward then me and I was fully follow her when she entered in the room directly I was also entered in the room, after enter in the room I had a fear of her elder auncle because who was not away from the city who was on busy his government school which was situated three kilometer away from the home. He any time can reported at his home that's why I was not fully psycologicaly liberated I had a pressure but when she closed the door and then offered me sweet and a glass of a water I was eaten the sweet and sip the glass of water than I was began to sucked her lips and her neck she became very lusty and she also began to sucked me I was also became more lusty and I made told her legs by back side and wanted to losed her virginity. I made her nude. But she remind me that her elder uncle can come any time. So I was released her, and wanted to released myself because I was more aggesive and lusty. But due to the fear of her uncle and basically a fear of our Self-respect, dignity I released her and told that moved for temple side I moved for temple and by cell phone convince her, I invited her for come in the temple she was committed for come in the temple So I wait for her in the temple it's a very famous temple of Gorakhpur every where was strict security no one could touch to his opposite gender but their were a probability that we could convince or talk to each other.

So after the waiting of half an hours she came and we meet in a restaurant where sip the many cup of coffee, the cofee was a excuse of our long conversation she was told me that she was very hungry for sexually satisfaction and she wanted to loosed her virginity with me and had a desire for enjoy the life of top pleasure but due to the fear of her elder uncle she could not allowed me for loosed her virginity. Because he could come at any time after listen her desire my sweet suddenly drop at my body because really I feel I am more lusty men on the earth and waiting for that time when I will loosed her virginity it will be a great gift for conversation my life. So when we began to our conversation that time a shining day's but when a shining day's was turn into dark evening we did not know but we know we wanted to enlarge the day's and a evening who never come and as like as made wanted to made eye glance forever we did not wanted to miss pointed to our eyes and realy her, eyes was so killing that evil's evening was frighten me and jooked on my self because with in few minutes my beautiful beloved will be gone away from my eyes so she told me for valediction. I never wanted to released her. But like every lover of the earth with the moist eyes I was valediction to her.

Within few minutes she was inivisible to my eyes and I began to journey of my home I arrived at my home at late night my mother was asked me about my monotonous I did not replied her. She offered me a cup of tea.

Then with nimbility I take dinner then moved for my bed room. Where I began to talk to Pinkee. She was told me that after arrived at late night in home, they were protested her, but by broad conversation they were became satisfied she was told me about a surprise that in next month a festival will be organised in her remote village so in that festival her involvement was very necessary, because her Mummy and other uncle at in her remote village requested her to visit that festival so her elder uncle agreed about her tour which will be held next month in her remote village. So she was very glad, because after arrival at her home she would easily meet with me that's why she offered me fifty to fifty five kiss on the all and first time she was very glad so began to talk to each other since 11.50 p.m. and watch was beeping at 4.30 a.m. in the morning. It's very long time and its very dangerous for us and I known but that was not my problem that a was a compulsion of my heart and my young age and now a day's we were became very open about each and every angle of our conversation we point outed about every thing a hour's to money hour's, we discuss about sex or normal education our life style each and every thing and I further it is also gradually we became very close to each other.

So after that meeting we did not wanted to made another mistake of meeting with each other because, it could became a very blunder mistake for us. So every thing we well known and every day we counted the day's of her arrival at her home, gradually the day's was decreasing to day by day but our conversation to each other was becoming cool it was increasing to day by day and we wait for our new meeting in her remote village, I was very glad because I had a secure future life partner, who was decent well educated, chasting and virgin and in Indian motherland or any where in the world the role of character is very important for any one if some one loosed million of rupees in one time its not blunder mistake and it's not great loss.

But if someone lost their charactr it means they lost everything because if you loose one time your character then you will lost the trust of people and if you will like to be a characterise person in the world so at that time you should be more deserve than other innocent people because already you had lost your trust on people, that's why every student every youngsters should be aware about their cutlture-custom and tradition and should be utilise their energy in the good work, never involve in any type of whoring gambling.

Alchohal drinking and if you want to search a beautiful girl so first you have to need make a beautiful career suddenly every beautiful girl will be slave of yourself so I am never against to do not make any girl friend make but do not play with her because it will be very difficult for you in your upcoming life that's why always remember. If you will do anything wrong so alway's will be ready for it's wrong result. So I had a very pure girl friend. Who will be my life partner.

So gradually a time was came for her attending a festival at her remote village. So her arrival was at her home, fully decided so I was also very glad because at that time was very near which I was waiting since long time because after meeting in the temple we made a long gap with in our next meeting's so it's a will be very pleasure experience for us and the day and night was became enlarge because we wanted to just change the day and night we wanted to meet with each other. So after waiting of the long time she came in her village attending for festival she made me a call my heart was very delighted and waiting for meeting with her every member of her family became very glad because rarely she came in her remote village because she never got a time from Gorakhpur. So she enjoyed in the festival and celebrated with each other she had very respect in her family because she had many responsibilities in Gorakhpur she was all in all virtual of her family in Gorakhpur that's why every member's of her family was fully trusted on herself.

So after her arrival at her remote village our convertsation with each other was not effected by the her family members in her remote village.

So once she made a plan for watching the movie because her remote village was situated on my locality area, easily I could meet with her.

So she told me that her friend Divya was also wanted to watch the movie but she will be join with her boy friend go a so she offered me a proposal because Divya was her good friends and without Divya her lonely journey of any where was not possible because their parents was so typical and traditional they never, allowed her. This type of opportunity, so she was told me every thing that she came with Divya from her town and I was join them when they came two kilometer away from their town.

I booked a Indica car for them and we sat in the back side of sit and my driver drive the car.

Gradually our car run in the jouney of love, peace and a couple of future life partner that was my very pleasure experience of life. Divya was so nice and charming girl and she was also very traditional we reported at Gorakhpur at 11 am in the morning where Divya's boy friends was all ready presented we parked the car then we met with boy friends of Divya who was not very handsome boy comparatively to Divya but he was really nice girls (boys) and he was also very traditional, because after entry in the theator we sit with consequently I was sit beside the Pinkee and I was physically very hunger because it's to long's time for our meeting, and one side their are no boundation of her elder uncle because she was came with Divya and she stayed in her remote village where her mother was all in all virtual for her. She could made excuse if she could not return before the evening because they made a excuse juarny for some thing urgent work So I feel mentain pleasure and very peace because in earlier time whenever she was stayed in Gorakhpur with her elder uncle she was very responsible for her domestic work and other responsibilities whenever she was met with me with in fifteen minutes always her mobile phone was keeping beeping that's why these type of problem always created but that day's there were no overburden of her call or any type of responsibilities of her domestic work or any other responsibilities so she was fully free from any type of boundation or strictness so after sitting besides with her. I began to sucking her lips because I spended long time in Chandigarh, Simla, Delhi, and Dehradun that's why these all thing was very minor for me, but those couple Divya and her boy friend they did not made any mistake and another thing is that they used a very sweet and clear, Hindi language and never touches to each other but I was by chance watched on the screen otherwise full time I was busy in the romance with Pinkee. She was also very lusty. and she had only shy to other audience than she told me that we should be control to your self because many audience made eye glance to us but further it is also in the whole movie I made a blunder romance and she was very satisfied to my romance with in watching the movie the shining day's was turn into dark evening that climate was winter season so we suddenly came back to return for our dewelling the boy friend of Divya was gone away, and we Pinkee, Divya, Atul and our driver came with our Indica car my driver was on the nice mood and he fast drive the Indica, but I was not made any complain against him.

Because I was very happy to my life and basically Pinkee because I lost chastity of a Indian Girl was not lost her virginity But their were not less value of her chastity I was fully committed to made her as a life partner the speed of our Indica was gradually stopped at the home town of Pinkee where I droped them than I take valediction to them, then my driver was young and his name was Jaishree Yadav after their drope we were very close to my home town so, the driver has drope me at besides my residence.

I was pay him his fee then I was entered in my home. I was stayed with my mother and my sister. so after arrival at the home. I freshed in the bathroom. Then I completed the dinner, than moved for my bed room where I began talk to the Pinkee. It was began at 10.30 p.m. to 4.30 a.m. the time early of calling because she was came from Gorakhpur and their are no any ouer burden for her thats why she became free at very early in the evening.

After one meeting to another meeting was not fade our physical and mental desire it was increasing to day by day. Gradually many day's and night was passed after that meeting and our physical desire that time was on the boom. So I wanted to concern her for next meeting and I was concern her, for another meeting but she was not agreed. So I became very angry against her, and I did not wanted talk to her because long meeting fully made me more lusty and addicted always I wanted to romance with her so she was convince me that she will made a journey of my sister home where easily we could meet with each other.

I was asked her how it may be possible at my sister home where my sister is always domenate me as a small kid's and if she I will find me in some thing guilty then what will happen she was convince me whenever every one sleep in the night then I will come with you, and that time no one could imagine of these type of activities she was replied me. I was convince her that our relation gradually going on sounding and gradually every one, understood can and it so in these condition my sister never will leave me alone because she is more conciousnes about my self she is more caring me than my mother and so if she will find in any guilty in me than she will be kill me. She was replyed that she will urgest every thing so according to our plan with in some day's she was made a journey of my sister home and earlier she was inform me. So I was also fearless and I was made a juarny of my sister home where she was all ready assemble after our arrival we made a eye glance with each other she was passed smile I was jumping it's a pleasure and royal experience of my life.

So after dinner every family member of my sleep but my sister at the mid night made security.

But after mid night she was also sleep and I was waiting for that golden opportunity then I made a golden night I was made a call and she waiting for my call suddenly she was pickup my call I invited her in my bedroom because I was alone sleep in the room and she was also alone sleep in another bedroom and after my invitation she was came in my room. I was very lusty and aggressive, and after her entry in the room I was closely stucked with her and began to sucked her lips she was also very lusty and began to sucked my lips I wanted to loosed her virginity because I was became very lusty and main thing is that her. Physical attraction was killed myself her parrot nose, rosy rosey, chuck star like eyes and moral lips was so killing and any real men of the world can not control to their self so I was not excapteation I began sucking her neck and lips and cheeks she was politely asked me you are really love me. I was told her do you have any doubt she was replied nothing.

I made her, nude and sucking her every thing that was very lusty night. She told me that if you are love me so please do not loosed my virginity. It was very hard for me. Because as a young strong men my controlling on my lusty body was impossible but she made me swear and I was really loved her that's why I was controlled on myself and sucked her every thing but released her without loosed her virginity she was made me commitment that loosed my virginity but after marriage I was accepted her. Proposal and relased her and after that's all the time was going on 3.30 a.m. of morning and then she was moved for bed room I was sleep that not with unconciousness because I could not completed my sexual desire but remine disere I was completed than in the early morning I was moved for my dwelling and with in two day's she was also moved for her remote village but after that incident we became more choser than previous time and every day's we began, conversation at the night time and finished at the right time we were very happy, then when she stayed at Gorakhpur but with in few day's for elder uncle call her for Gorakhpur she did not wanted to gone away from their parents but it's was compulsion of her mother because she had fine girl and her uncle was guardian of every one in the family thats why She could not gone away from the ordered of her elder uncle so she was gone a with her cousin in the Gorakhpur for cure of her elder uncle, aunty and her cousin and my nephew their were on problem was a very big that only two bed room and many time the number of people was increasing of eight so urgestment was not so easy but Pinkee was very innocent and decent without any complain she alway's acclimatsize herself on the basis of her elder uncle and their families.

She did not wanted to stayed in Gorakhpur but it was compulsion after her arrival in Gorakhpur according to my right time I made a call to Pinkee.

She picked my call and began talk to me with in our long conversation unthrealed as in more attachment to each other, so we became fully open for each other.

I began talk to her that night I was very lusty. I did not known why but first time I asked question to her that you are virgin or not she was told me what happen and why your asking this type of ridiculous question. I was replied nothing but honestly answered me she was told me that. I never made any journey away from my home and any outsider's is not allowed for entry in my home. So how it may be possible that.

I did not asked any question more once upon a time in the school of my nephew as decided that parents teacher's meeting's where guardian arrival was necessary but unfortunately my brother-in-law did not had more time who was busy in his office work. So my brother-in-law was advice me for attend that meeting.

So I made a journey of master ji home, where I was received by my nephew Suraj then we were moved for his school.

So I was in a journey of my self responsibility in his school as a gurdian and laterly I was came back to return at masterji home, where I was seen. Masterji was coloured his hair and clean saved carefully every hair of his chest. His chest was so clean and he was clean saved his moustache and beard.

He fully tried to became a young man but he was looking like a old man but who was best trying for his battle against his old age. Master ji was more than fifty six year's old.

When I was entered in his home he tried wear a blue T Shirt of Levis.

It's a totally fashion of young generation besides his chair his wife was sit at the bed his wife was so old lady and who was looke like more than sixty five year. I was seen master ji before ten year's ago when I was in a very early age but that time master ji was very simple man that time who weared the very simple clothes and mentain his moustache. I mean when he was at the age forty seven he was very simple innocent and decent and he was fully vegetarian but with in five year's master ji was involve in the drinking, gambling and tried to look like a young man whenever I was entered in his room, that his every activities was very silence his under wear was from jocky company but in semi urban areas merely a old people listen the name of these all brand I stayed a long time in urban India and with in officer of Indian Army where every thing was learned how a mysteries can solve in realism.

I saw master ji with very carefully then entered in another room where my nephew and Pinkee was sit she looked me and passed smile I was predicament in the activities of that home in the presence of master ji that time I became very consiousness and activities between master ji and Pinkee they did not talk to each other in my presence after that's I came with my nephew and moved for his school where I follow that's all formalities but many arguments questions put up in my brain. Because I was very consiousness about Pinkee, after that incident I carefully point out to every activities of Pinkee, and I made I call in 11.30 p.m. she was told me that every night she bathing and take her teeth brush than I remind in her remote village time she never. Did any brush or bathing in the night. So why she bathing and did her brush in mid night why? and in many time whenever I call her in mid night litsten the voice of her elder uncle if her elder uncle had any problem so never convince to her wife he alway's share his every problem to Pinkee and Pinkee was loved me and she had many complain to her famile member and mostly complain to her auntee but she had never any complain to her elder uncle she alway's told me that her elder uncle is so fine person and he is only crossing the age of five six but he have mostly friend of young generation. Many time I made a joke against her elder uncle but she became angry against me she was told me that my uncle is very nice person.

I was asked many person to when master ji began his drinking these all relatives of master ji was told me that with in five year's and his hair colour who's every relative was told me that's his every demerit of his life began to within five years, and then I was asked them how much duration happen to of Pinkee stayed in Gorakhpur they were told me five years, I had every answer of every question which was argue in my mind.

When I made a call in mid night many times she was talk to her elder uncle.

And after note these all activities of both directly I was asked her you are virgin she was told me yes.

I was replied I would like to physically relation with you because you are not cycle riding and you are not active in the sports so you should be preserve your hyphen and after relation it will be clear after listen these statement she hesitated. I asked her politely that tell me every thing clearly because I like loyalty and honesty if you are true speaker I will sympathy on yourself and forget your every mistakes she began to crying on cell phone told that she have sexually relation to her elder uncle since last five year's ago and every day he wanted to raped me but due to his physical weakness many time failed in his desire and many times became successful. She was crying and continued that I did not wanted to live more day's in the world because I lost every thing by him. I convince her then.

She was told me when she came from her remote village to semi urban city in Gorakhpur she was at the age of eighteen and did not have maturity once he came in night and forced ford. For rape that time she was ignore but he frightend her so with in compulsion of young age she became involve in the vangeful and sin activities and loosed her virginity, chestity and dignity I was shocked and wanted to killed myself because how it may be possible in the Indian society a real uncle can rape of his real niece and their activities continued within five year's but any family member how could not know. These type of hated activites of a bludder mistakes and Himalyan blunder mistake of society she was told me that she wanted to save her dignity and with in fear of her honour she was not share to anyone and it any time she wanted told that's all incident the her family member. Always justified him as very decent and innocent. So I had a answer of my every question, why these all seven brother was not quarrel to each other that time I was realised that I was engaged with her. But I never feel she really loved me because earlier I had a experience of chisting girl friend who alway's concentrate on myself who those all spiritually loved me these love was not for profession or greed for becoming a life partner but mentality of pinke was only for her security forever for her life. But I feel that she loved her auncle without any restriction of marriage she always care him as a beloved or life partner because every one of her family member was told that she is very careful for her uncle.

And she was accepted thats all hated activities that's no any place in the Indian society I was very very aggressive and break down with internal soul where is gone, my Indian girl, and their tradition, culture and custom. Her elder uncle was a teacher of Sanskrit it's a very holly unique and first language of India, may be every Hindusm epic written in this holly language it's do not have any direct or indirect relation to western language so I hope he is specialist in Sanskrit mean should be dominate the Indian culture because who is a orator of Sanskrit every student and common people have a hope and trust of salvation to him because who is brahaman mean I leader of society. In the ancient time every thing was right if brahaman think it is right, the brihaman were treated as a god or as a massanger of god no doult many brahaman deserved for it.

That's why they secure reverene for them and these community. So what A Sanskrit teacher and brahaman who crosses above of middle age but physically used his nephew as a prostitute and she was in compulsion of poverty because her father was psycologically ill and her mother had a responsibilities of five sisters, her uncle everyday raped her why because who have no fear to constitution of India and scholar of law and order of justice so what every Indian should be follow him or punish him make a strong voice against domestic violence. How I could trust to he self. She could not defend her dignity chastity to her elder uncle she was unable to protested against her elder uncle who crossed the middle age of fifty six but she was at twenty but laterly she became habitual of his fade last.

She made his every night lusty without inferior feeling about her virginity and chastity by force she was aggreed to told me that's all indeed incident with the promise of marry with her I was commited to make a life partner her.

But I was born in a cultured brahaman family where recognised the western education western, cloth's western institution for for further studies western instrument for research western style for game because they are more advance to us in these all but my family never recognised a girl who fell down to a relation with a old man, who was her real elder uncle. According to Indian culture, custom and tradition it's a great sin's.

If you become a prosperous person and have a aristocratic life so it's not mean you should be play with a poor girl.

They sended her in a hope a golden future of a rural unmature fair slim parrot nose a beautiful girl at a dwelling of her uncle who dwell with his wife and nephew who's nephew was a student of B.Sc. medical so who almost busy on his study who was taken coaching that's why full day s who stayed awayed from home. Alway's came back to return in evening after arrival became tired and did not wanted to waste time and with in few hour's of study who prefer a deeply sleep.

And the wife of Ramesh was psycologicaly ill woman so she take a sleeping piles so in any condition in night she could not awake in night and Mr. Ramesh take a benefit of this condition and made entry in the room of Pinkee and closely touches her body she is very beautiful but she was in the complusion of poverty and socked how he can it.

Because he is my guardian and real uncle but Mr Ramesh was convine her she's the greed of money made her greedy so gradually she also became a habitual of his relation he made his every night lusty she was at twenty year old and came with her virginity and chastity but a real elder uncle loosed or spoil her virginity and chastity with in few day's he became habitual and ill treated with his wife and whenever his wife return in her consiousness and made a vulgur comments in these pure Indian relation on which billion of Indian people blinding trust. That was became corrupt the Pinkee and her elder uncle became angry and abused his wife and Mr. Ramesh organised a planning that and convince Pinkee to make ridiculous activities against his wife like whenever the some people gathered on home and she lived alone if no one could seen them in that condition she should throughn some drop of water because the effect of water she would by cry and abuse her so people easily could trust on her self that she is essentric and Pinkee alway's applied it and with in few day's her cousin brother also involve in the vulgar joke with his elder auntee because he is totally unware the condition that what happening with them After known these all hated sin's incident I was inform in her family.

Her remain family member's who stayed in her remote village. So after knowing her condition they so removed her from her elder uncle her did not wanted to leave her, but really she migrated from his home and I was inform to every one about this notiee activities in her family member they known they removed her but they did not take any necessary action against him.

The mother of Pinkee was totally against of my battle for truth she only focused on her uncle income and discribe about the merit of Mr. Ramesh she known everything that he raped her daughter with last with in five years but she became shylock only for money, I was loved Pinkee with my internal soul her chastity and her honour in society was my first target man makes money but money never makes a man I was in a great afraid and it was lunacy. I was fully disconected and drowned in ocean of griel how she can it she alway's give me a another excuse and counting the merit of her elder uncle but I was matured in civilise family where honour dignity and self respect is everything the value of money is nothing because if I have a idea and wisdom I can be a millionaire with in few year's that's why every incident arounded in my nervous system. It was very painful time of my life how it was happened I did not known.

What is going on in Indian culture due to financial crisis a niece sarve her uncle as a prostitute he spended the money not for his blood relation. But for his physically sexually satisfaction. Every one is aware about their hated activities but no one argue to old man regard's this hated activities. Why what is the value of money above than a dignity of Indian girl how much cheap cast the expanse of our country girl. One sides politicians fulfil their bank and one side a unique beautifull girl loosed her shy dignity, chastity, virginity only for money.

Where is our social reformer and where is our law scholar.

Had I known the pain of the mysteries of modern relation I would have cried from door to door do not send your daughter to the home of any relatives.